St. Kitts-Nevis

WORLD BIBLIOGRAPHICAL SERIES

General Editors:
Robert G. Neville (Executive Editor)
John J. Horton

Robert A. Myers   Hans H. Wellisch
Ian Wallace   Ralph Lee Woodward, Jr.

John J. Horton is Deputy Librarian of the University of Bradford and currently Chairman of its Academic Board of Studies in Social Sciences. He has maintained a longstanding interest in the discipline of area studies and its associated bibliographical problems, with special reference to European Studies. In particular he has published in the field of Icelandic and of Yugoslav studies, including the two relevant volumes in the World Bibliographical Series.

Robert A. Myers is Associate Professor of Anthropology in the Division of Social Sciences and Director of Study Abroad Programs at Alfred University, Alfred, New York. He has studied post-colonial island nations of the Caribbean and has spent two years in Nigeria on a Fulbright Lectureship. His interests include international public health, historical anthropology and developing societies. In addition to *Amerindians of the Lesser Antilles: a bibliography* (1981), *A Resource Guide to Dominica, 1493-1986* (1987) and numerous articles, he has compiled the World Bibliographical Series volumes on *Dominica* (1987), *Nigeria* (1989) and *Ghana* (1991).

Ian Wallace is Professor of German at the University of Bath. A graduate of Oxford in French and German, he also studied in Tübingen, Heidelberg and Lausanne before taking teaching posts at universities in the USA, Scotland and England. He specializes in contemporary German affairs, especially literature and culture, on which he has published numerous articles and books. In 1979 he founded the journal *GDR Monitor*, which he continues to edit under its new title *German Monitor*.

Hans H. Wellisch is Professor emeritus at the College of Library and Information Services, University of Maryland. He was President of the American Society of Indexers and was a member of the International Federation for Documentation. He is the author of numerous articles and several books on indexing and abstracting, and has published *The Conversion of Scripts and Indexing and Abstracting: an International Bibliography*, and *Indexing from A to Z*. He also contributes frequently to *Journal of the American Society for Information Science*, *The Indexer* and other professional journals.

Ralph Lee Woodward, Jr. is Professor of History at Tulane University, New Orleans. He is the author of *Central America, a Nation Divided*, 2nd ed. (1985), as well as several monographs and more than seventy scholarly articles on modern Latin America. He has also compiled volumes in the World Bibliographical Series on *Belize* (1980), *El Salvador* (1988), *Guatemala* (Rev. Ed.) (1992) and *Nicaragua* (Rev. Ed.) (1994). Dr. Woodward edited the Central American section of the *Research Guide to Central America and the Caribbean* (1985) and is currently associate editor of Scribner's *Encyclopedia of Latin American History*.

VOLUME 174

St. Kitts-Nevis

Verna Penn Moll

CLIO PRESS

OXFORD, ENGLAND · SANTA BARBARA, CALIFORNIA
DENVER, COLORADO

British Library Cataloguing in Publication Data

St. Kitts-Nevis. – (World Bibliographical
series; vol. 174)
I. Moll, V. Penn   II. Series
016.972973

ISBN 1–85109–222–6

ABC-CLIO Ltd.,
Old Clarendon Ironworks,
35A Great Clarendon Street,
Oxford OX2 6AT, England.

———————

ABC-CLIO Inc.,
130 Cremona Drive,
Santa Barbara,
CA 93116, USA.

Designed by Bernard Crossland.
Typeset by Columns Design and Production Services Ltd, Reading, England.
Printed and bound in Great Britain by
Bookcraft (Bath) Ltd., Midsomer Norton.

THE WORLD BIBLIOGRAPHICAL SERIES

This series, which is principally designed for the English speaker, will eventually cover every country (and many of the world's principal regions), each in a separate volume comprising annotated entries on works dealing with its history, geography, economy and politics; and with its people, their culture, customs, religion and social organization. Attention will also be paid to current living conditions – housing, education, newspapers, clothing, etc.– that are all too often ignored in standard bibliographies; and to those particular aspects relevant to individual countries. Each volume seeks to achieve, by use of careful selectivity and critical assessment of the literature, an expression of the country and an appreciation of its nature and national aspirations, to guide the reader towards an understanding of its importance. The keynote of the series is to provide, in a uniform format, an interpretation of each country that will express its culture, its place in the world, and the qualities and background that make it unique. The views expressed in individual volumes, however, are not necessarily those of the publisher.

VOLUMES IN THE SERIES

To the Stevens (Penn) family and all families
of St. Kitts-Nevis

Contents

Contents

Contents

Contents

Introduction

The Federation of St. Christopher (more commonly known as St. Kitts) and Nevis is situated in the eastern Caribbean Sea, at the northern end of the Leeward Island chain about one-third of the way between Puerto Rico and Trinidad and Tobago. The islands lie approximately between 17° north latitude and 62° west longitude. They are sometimes referred to as 'the bat and ball', St. Kitts being oval in shape with a long neck of land extending like a handle from the southeastern tip. It is separated from the more 'rounded' Nevis by three miles of Caribbean sea.

The Federation covers a total area of 101 square miles (St. Kitts 65, Nevis 36), and enjoys a subtropical climate tempered by constant sea breezes. There is little seasonal variation in temperature but the rainy season lasts from May to November. The terrain is volcanic with mountainous interiors and fertile valleys. Mineral resources are negligible but arable land, permanent crops, meadows and pastures, forest and woodland, occupy about fifty-nine per cent of the total acreage.

St. Kitts and Nevis cherish a rich and varied history. The Indians' 'Liamuiga' (fertile isle) was renamed St. Christopher (St. Kitts for short) by Columbus in 1493 and became Britain's first colony in the West Indies in 1623. Nevis was subsequently settled in 1628 by planters from St. Kitts. The French followed the British to St. Kitts and destroyed the English colony there in 1666. Nevis then became the most important and prosperous of the Leeward Islands for many years. However, the British returned to St. Kitts, and the British and French antagonized each other for one hundred and fifty years of fierce battles, until in 1783, when the Treaty of Versailles formally acknowledged British sovereignty. Because of its renowned fort at Brimstone Hill, St. Kitts is often referred to as Britain's Gibraltar in the West Indies.

Nevis, birthplace of Alexander Hamilton, Fanny Nisbet (wife of Horatio Nelson, who was the enforcement officer of the Treaty of

Versailles) continued to prosper. The Leeward Islands Governor John Hart had recommended a union of Nevis and St. Kitts in 1724; Anguilla joined St. Kitts in 1816, but it was not until the end of 1882 that Nevis and St. Kitts were united, the three islands forming one presidency of St. Kitts-Nevis-Anguilla.

The islands formed part of the Leeward Islands Federation from 1871 to 1956 and part of the West Indian Federation from 1958 to 1962 when the Federation was dissolved. A constitution in 1960 provided for government through an Administrator and an enlarged Legislative Council.

Associated Statehood with the United Kingdom was achieved in 1967, giving the islands full internal autonomy, with the United Kingdom retaining responsibility for defence and foreign relations. Anguilla seceded from the union in 1970 after a peaceful rebellion.

Robert Bradshaw, leader of the Labour Party formed in 1932, became the State's first Premier. Disagreements over constitutional advancement in the House of Assembly led to civil disturbances and industrial unrest in 1983 but St. Kitts-Nevis gained independence from Britain in the same year, and became a full member of the Commonwealth of Nations. The Constitution adopted on 19 September 1983 describes the nation as a 'sovereign democratic federated State', with Queen Elizabeth II as head of the monarchy (represented by the Governor-General); the Premier; and Executive and Legislative Councils. The Legislature is operated by a unicameral House of Assembly.

Since 1983 Nevis has had its own legislature, Premier, legislation and administration. The Nevis Island Administration has administrative responsibility for Nevis's communications, education, natural resources, fisheries, health and welfare, labour and licensing of imports and exports. The Constitution also provides for the secession of Nevis from the Federation. Independence Day, 19 September (1983), is observed as an annual National holiday on both islands.

There are four political parties. The St. Kitts and Nevis Labour Party (SKNLP), led in turn by Bradshaw, Paul Southwell and Lee Moore, governed from 1969-1980. The other parties are: the People's Action Movement (PAM), led by Dr Kennedy Simmonds; the Nevis Reformation Party (NRP) led by Simeon Daniel; and the Concerned Citizens Movement (CCM), led by Vance Amory. In the general elections of 1980, the PAM/NRP coalition government was formed under Premier Kennedy Simmonds, and returned to power in subsequent general elections, in 1984, 1989 and 1993. The precise results of the 1993 general elections were as follows: People's Action

Movement, 4 seats; Labour Party, 4 seats; Concerned Citizens' Movement, 2 seats; and the Nevis Reformation Party, 1 seat. A coalition of the PAM and NRP was again formed, but the opposition parties and various sectors of the community called for fresh elections.

The legal system is based on English common law. Justice is administered by the Eastern Caribbean Supreme Court, whose headquarters are to be found in St. Lucia, and consists of a Court of Appeal and a High Court. One of the Puisne judges is resident in St. Kitts. The Magistrate Courts deal with minor and civil offences.

The total population of the Federation of St. Christopher-Nevis is approximately 44,000 (Europa yearbook 1994), with a growth rate of 0.59 per cent, a birth rate of 23.93 births per 1,000 population and a death rate of 10.39 deaths per 1,000 population. The infant mortality rate is 20.5 deaths per 1,000 live births and the fertility rate is 2.64 children born per woman. The people are English-speaking with a literacy rate of 98 per cent. Practising religions are Anglican, various Protestant sects, and Roman Catholic. The net migration rate in 1993 was 7.67 migrants per 1,000 population.

The twin-island state has always welcomed regional economic development and integration. The inaugural meeting of the Organisation of Eastern Caribbean States was held in Basseterre, St. Kitts in 1981, and the Honourable Kennedy A. Simmonds and Vaughan Lewis have served in leading positions in the Organisation. The headquarters of the Caribbean Development Bank is also based in Basseterre. The state has membership in several regional and international associations, e.g. African Caribbean Pacific countries (ACP); Caribbean Community and Common Market (CARICOM); Economic Commission for Latin America and the Caribbean (ECLAC); Food and Agricultural Organisation (FAO); International Monetary Fund (IMF); INTERPOL; Organisation of American States (OAS); Organisation of Eastern Caribbean States (OECS); United Nations (UN); United Nations Conference on Trade and Industry (UNCTAD); United Nations Educational Scientific and Cultural Organisation (UNESCO); World Health Organisation (WHO); and many other international bodies.

The economy of the Federation is traditionally agro-based, including forestry and fishing, but primarily cultivating and processing sugar cane as the principal cash crop. On Nevis sea-island cotton is grown and coconuts exported.

Developments in regional and international markets, coupled with new government policy, have led to diversifying agriculture by producing crops to replace imports, for example, rice and coffee. Imports, which mainly consist of foodstuffs, intermediate manufactures, machinery and fuels totalled EC $103.2 million in 1990. During the 1980s, export-oriented manufacturing and tourism assumed larger roles; other export commodities include clothing, foot wear, electronics, postage stamps, beer and other beverages.

The country conducts 53 per cent of its trade with the United States of America; 22 per cent with the United Kingdom; 5 per cent with Trinidad and Tobago; and 5 per cent with the Organisation of Eastern Caribbean States. A 1994 report on the condition of the Caribbean sugar industry (written by Canute James, and entitled *Sugar industries respond to adversity*, Financial Times, June 24, 1994, p. 28), states that St. Kitts-Nevis, the smallest producer in the Commonwealth Caribbean, was the only one to record an increase in production. Remittances from overseas workers also aid the economy. With a labour force of approximately 20,000, the National product real growth was 6.8 per cent in 1991 and EC $3,500 per capita. The inflation rate was 4.2 per cent in 1991, while the unemployment rate was 12.2 per cent and the external debt, $37.2 million.

The communications infrastructure has recently been enhanced by the construction of a road which opens up access to the South Eastern peninsular of St. Kitts, and by the improved facility of the airport, now accommodating direct flights from the United States of America. Telecommunications have been upgraded with good inter-island VHF/UHF/SHF radio connections and international links. Broadcast stations include two AM, and several television stations.

In an effort to control the development of tourism, specific areas, including Frigate Bay and the uninhabited Southern Peninsular, have been targeted for the building of condominiums and hotel accommodation.

The nation's distinctive cultural history is destined to be preserved, as the government has recently designated one square mile of Basseterre an historical zone where buildings are to be restored and new ones restricted, in order to maintain the traditional Caribbean style. Brimstone Hill Fortress on St. Kitts (for which the British and French fought for more than a century) is now a national park under a National Conservation and Environment Act intended to protect areas of natural beauty and historic interest.

St. Kitts and Nevis, like many other islands in the Caribbean, have suffered the loss of valuable records through hurricanes, fires and other disasters, but an effort is currently being made to preserve what remains. The Museum of Nevis History, formerly the Alexander Hamilton Museum, possesses an impressive collection of archives, including manuscripts, newspapers, maps, prints and stamps dating back to the 17th century, and staff members envisage further training to aid the enhancement of existing services. The Government Archives in St. Kitts are being maintained in a temperature-controlled room and plans are being made for training and procuring professional staff to administer the collection. Archives dating back to 1777 are also maintained by the St. Kitts Sugar Factory and Corporation, and by the Methodist, Anglican and Moravian Churches. The recently formed St. Christopher (St. Kitts) Heritage Society aims to ensure the continued development of historical discussion, discovery and preservation of that which is vitally relevant for building national cultural identity and international understanding and respect.

This unique culture emerged out of the multi-racial population of 17th-century Europeans, Africans and Amerindians. One writer claims that the 'folklore is the result of a syncretic coming together of African and European traditions'. This is clearly evident today in the special Christmas sports acted out in 'masquerade' and 'mummies' each year.

Education grades from primary to tertiary levels, with thirty-two primary schools, seven secondary, two vocational and a University of the West Indies centre. St. Kitts and Nevis boasts nationals of international acclaim in various disciplines. They are good ambassadors for their country and for the Caribbean region as a whole, also contributing significantly to the adopted countries in which they reside. The prolific novelist, Caryl Phillips, a Kittitian brought up in England, springs to mind. His novel, *Crossing the river*, published in 1993, spans 250 years of African diaspora and of relations between black and white. It won the James Tait Black Memorial prize and was short-listed for the Booker Prize. The gifted Rupert Gilchrist of Nevis, also living in England, has created for us the engaging *Dragonard* series. Professor of Economics Simon Jones-Hendrickson of the University of the United States Virgin Islands, writes and publishes journal articles, monographs and books on finance, economics and health. The late Hope R. Stevens, a New York lawyer of St. Kitts-Nevis roots, was instrumental in founding the British Virgin Islands Civic League in 1938, which petitioned the colonial administration to restore an elected Legislative Council in the British Virgin Islands. Joseph Archibald Q.C., a Kittitian, is president of the BVI Bar Association and holds official posts in several regional associations.

The bibliography

The present work is arranged according to the classification system of the World Bibliographical Series. Each entry has a running number, and within each chapter, entries are arranged in alphabetical sequences by title as far as possible. Works which are wholly and specifically about St. Kitts-Nevis are integrated with general titles which bear significant relevance to the islands, as are works which treat Nevis singularly. A list of those theses which are not annotated in the main work is included in the preliminary pages.

This bibliography details and evaluates 565 selected sources, and is intended to assist users in understanding the people of St. Kitts and Nevis and their culture. Aspects of the history, geography, politics, social-cultural and economic conditions of these islands are covered, making this a key work of reference, which should be invaluable to students, librarians, business people and general readers.

Verna Penn Moll
November 1994.

Acknowledgements

I have tapped the resources of many individuals, libraries and data bases. Among them are: the libraries of St. Kitts and Nevis; the Organisation of Eastern Caribbean States: Economic Affairs Secretariat; the University of the West Indies, Kingston, Jamaica; Island Resources Foundation; British Virgin Islands Public Library; Enid Baa Public Library; the Ralph Paiwonsky Library (University of US Virgin Islands); Royal Commonwealth Society Collection (Cambridge University Library); the Centre for Caribbean Studies (University of Warwick); the High Commission for Eastern Caribbean States, UK; the Sloman Collection of the University of Essex; the Miami Public Library; University Microfilms International; the British Library; the Commonwealth Secretariat; and the inter-loan and document delivery services of my local Colchester Public Library.

Special mention of assistance received is gratefully recorded for the following persons: Val P. Sargeant; Claudette de Freitas; Delnora Baley; Terry A. Barringer; Edward L. Towle; Iris Romney; Patricia Dunn; Theresa Lianzi; Manoj Veghala; Jackson Karunasekera; and Julia Goddard.

However, when promised assistance failed and it was disheartening to go on, the encouragement of my husband, Peter, proved vital to the completion of this book and to him I am most grateful.

Theses and Dissertations on St. Kitts-Nevis

S. Barett. 'The sugar industry of St. Kitts-Nevis: the post-war experience', BA thesis, University of the West Indies, Jamaica, 1985.

Edris Learice Bird. 'University adult education and development: a case study of three Caribbean Islands – Antigua, St. Kitts and Montserrat', Ed dissertation, University of Toronto, 1981.

Vincent O'Mahony Cooper. 'Basilectal creole, decreolization, and autonomous language change in St. Kitts-Nevis', PhD dissertation, Princeton University, 1979.

Edward Locksley Cox. 'The shadow of freedom: freedmen in the slave societies of Grenada and St. Kitts, 1763-1833', PhD dissertation, Johns Hopkins University, 1977.

Diana Angela Demay. 'The St. Kitts mental health system: a sociological analysis of St. Kitts', PhD dissertation, University of California, 1989.

Phyllis Harriet Fleming. 'The bitter of the sweet: sugar production and under-development on St. Kitts', PhD dissertation, Carleton University, 1988.

Richard Frucht. 'Community and context in a colonial society: social and economic change in Nevis, British West Indies', PhD dissertation, Brandeis University, 1966.

R. Christopher Goodwin. 'The prehistoric cultural ecology of St, Kitts, West Indies: a case study in island archeology', PhD dissertation, Arizona State University, 1989.

Judith Danford Gussler. 'Nutritional implications of food distribution networks in St. Kitts', PhD dissertation, Ohio State University, 1975.

Stanley Keith Henry. 'Place of culture of migrant Afro-West Indians in the political life of Black New York in the period 1918 to 1966', PhD dissertation, University of Toronto, 1973.

A. Hobson. 'An appraisal of the water supply system in St. Kitts', BA thesis, University of the West Indies, 1990.

J. R. V. Johnston. 'The sugar plantation of the heirs of Lady Frances Stapleton, 1746-1810', MA thesis, University of Wales, 1965.

Catherine Joy Jones. 'Immigration and social adjustment: a case study of West Indian food habits in London', PhD dissertation, University of London, 1971.

Simon Jones-Hendrickson. 'The dynamics of the labour market for nurses from the Commonwealth Caribbean,' PhD dissertation, University of Exeter, 1976.

Carolyn Libird. 'Contraceptive use in Nevis', BA thesis, University of the West Indies, n.d.

P. Martin-Kaye. 'The double arc of the Lesser Antilles', PhD thesis, University of London, 1960.

Brian Lawrence Maze. 'The selective utilisation of legal avenues of assistance by women on the Caribbean island of St. Kitts in the British Leewards', PhD dissertation, Ohio State University, 1985.

Mary Cathey Maze. 'Adult male immature interactions in a captive group of St. Kitts vervets (Cercopithecus aethiops): a comparison with adult female immature dyads (Paternalism)', PhD dissertation, Ohio State University, 1985.

Gordon Clark Merrill. 'The historical geography of St. Kitts and Nevis, British West Indies', PhD dissertation, University of California, 1957.

Jeff Bacon Million. 'Rhizobium-related constraints to grain legume production in St. Kitts, West Indies', PhD dissertation, University of Florida, 1987.

Frank Leroy Mills. 'The development of alternative farming systems and prospects for change in the structure of agriculture in St. Kitts, West Indies', PhD dissertation, Clark University, 1974.

Frank Mills. 'The dual structure of agriculture in St. Kitts', MA thesis, University of Western Ontario, 1971.

Hope Bradley Richardson. 'A model of peer teacher in-service training for St. Kitts, West Indies', Ed dissertation, Yeshiva University, 1984.

Ralph Jerome Rauch. 'Some sociological determinants of a mental health programme on the islands of St. Kitts', PhD dissertation, Yale University, 1958.

Margaret Deanne Rouse-Jones. 'St. Kitts, 1713-1763: a study of the development of a plantation economy', PhD dissertation, Johns Hopkins University, 1979.

Sandra Smith. 'Genetic variation between demes of geographically separated African green monkeys (Cercopithecus Aethiops, St. Kitts-Nevis)', MSc thesis, McGill University, 1991.

David Richter Stevenson. 'Medicinal plant use and high blood pressure on St. Kitts, West Indies', PhD dissertation, Ohio State University, 1979.

H. Tempany. 'Cane syrups or fancy molasses: the composition of Antigua and St. Kitts molasses', PhD dissertation, University of London, 1914.

D. Thomas. 'West India merchants and planters in the eighteenth century, with special reference to St. Kitts', MA thesis, University of Kent, 1967.

Robert P. Waterman. 'Two old French poems on St. Leu and Saint Christopher from manuscript B.N. Francais 1555', PhD dissertation, Yale University, 1948.

Arthur P. Watts. 'Nevis and St. Christopher, 1782-1784', PhD dissertation, Université de Paris, 1925.

The Country and Its People

1 **Caribbean companion: the A-Z reference.**
Brian Dyde. London; Basingstoke, England: Macmillan Caribbean, 1992. 181p. map.

Any reader with an interest in the region is provided here with comprehensive information on a great variety of topics to do with the Caribbean. The work is arranged in alphabetical order and also covers the South American Caribbean, i.e. Guyana, Suriname and French Guiana. An introduction to St. Kitts-Nevis begins on page 143.

2 **Caribbean handbook, 1990.**
Edited by Jeremy Taylor. St. Johns, Antigua: Financial Times Caribbean, 1990. 260p. maps.

The editorial introduction focuses on general West Indian history, banking, telecommunications, Caribbean Community (Caricom), currencies, and tourism. Country by country summaries are provided including one for St. Kitts-Nevis.

3 **Caribbean islands handbook.**
Sara Cameron, Ben Box. London: Trade & Travel, 1993. 864p. maps.

Treats the islands objectively, St. Kitts-Nevis appearing on pages 401-18. The information is precise and interesting accounts of history, economics and finance, flora and fauna, beaches and water systems, sports and festivals are given. The details of excursions around St. Kitts and Nevis, and the specific information for visitors, covering transportation, food and drink, shopping, banks, health, security and tourist offices, all combine to make this a very useful item for tourists.

4 **Caribbean: the Lesser Antilles.**
   Edited by David Schwab.   Orchard Point, Singapore: APA Ltd., 1988.
   373p. (Insight Guides).

The guide covers all the islands in the Lesser Antilles group, including the Leeward Islands of which St. Kitts-Nevis are a part. It provides information on communication, holidays, accommodation and activities in each of these islands. Well illustrated in colour, the guide includes an informed article on St. Kitts-Nevis, which appears on p. 170-85.

5 **The Commonwealth yearbook, 1992.**
   Commonwealth Secretariat.   London: HMSO, 1992. 541p. map.

A compendium of information about the geography, climate, communications, economics, history and constitution of countries in the Commonwealth. It is arranged in seven parts, with an alphabetical arrangement of member countries in part four. Pages 314-316 focus on St. Christopher and Nevis, with a general introduction, followed by a résumé of the islands' history and constitution, land policy and government.

6 **The dancing sisters.**
   Marina Warner.   *Travel Holiday*, vol. 174 (February 1991), p. 63-71.

Warner illustrates how St. Kitts and Nevis still move to their own rhythms in this fascinating article. There are sections on natural history, vegetation, crops and fruits, and settlement. The historic Bath Hotel and Montpelier Plantation Inn on Nevis are described and an engaging explanation of how the Creole culture is emerging is offered. New developments on the islands include: the resorts of Frigate Bay and Jack Tar Village; Cane Spirited Rothschild rum that is being distilled for export and tourist consumption; and the golden Super Highway, a new road which winds for six and a half miles along the southern peninsula. Kit Kittle's photographs show the burial place of Sir Thomas Warner on St. Kitts; the Golden Lemon on St. Kitts; St. George's Anglican Church; Rawlins Plantation with its refurbished windmill guest house; a cricket match; and other scenic views of both islands.

7 **Essay on St. Kitts-Nevis.**
   Simon Jones-Hendrickson.   In: *Latin American and Caribbean contemporary record.*   Edited by Jack Hopkins.   New York: Holmes & Meir, 1984, p. 746-81. bibliog.

Written almost a decade ago by 'a son of the soil', this article is still relevant as an introduction to the unique charm of St. Kitts-Nevis, and to a general understanding of the cultural, social, economical and political life of the country.

8 **Europa world yearbook, 1994.**
   London: Europa Publications Ltd., 1994. 2 vols.

This work is a survey and reference guide to over 200 countries and territories, arranged in two volumes. Volume 1 gives details of international organizations and volume 2 of individual countries. There are introductory and statistical surveys and a directory relating to St. Christopher and Nevis on p. 2526-32.

9 **The independent way for St. Kitts.**
   Felix Redmill. *Geographical Magazine*, vol. 55, no. 12 (1983), p. 636-40.
Sets St. Kitts in its historical context and also highlights the contemporary, cultural style of its carnival and masquerade. The diversification of industry and new manufactures are outlined.

10 **Island profile: serenity in St. Kitts.**
   David Yeadon. *Caribbean Travel and Life*, vol. 9, no. 1 (Jan./Feb. 1994), p. 66-75. map.
Yeadon describes his encounter with the Kittitian way of life, at a time when islanders were celebrating a decade of independence from Britain. His experiences include: conversations with island hoteliers who relate the problems caused by hurricanes; visits to beautiful inns and plantation houses and to old churches, crammed with Sunday worshippers; and a taste of the island cuisine, which boasts such dishes as ginger chicken with breadfruit fritters and fresh mango ice cream. The beauty of the Mount Liamuiga trail is evoked, with its cascades of vines and ferns, bamboo clusters, heliconia blooms, cabbage palms and 350 year-old banyan trees. The author sees St. Kitts as an island steeped in history, illustrated by his numerous colour photographs of forts, sugar mills, plantation houses and churches. St. Kitts, he observes, 'still boasts an old-time West Indian charm.'

11 **Nevis: queen of the Leewards.**
   Maynard Good Stoddard. *Saturday Evening Post*, (May/June, 1985), p. 82-86.
Gives a warm and friendly introduction to the island, and, reflecting on its historic past, describes the mineral springs which used to be the hub of Nevis social life.

12 **Now hear the word of the Lord.**
   Cindy Selby. *Financial Times Weekend*, (29/30 June 1991), p.19.
'If you are ever in the Caribbean on Sunday, be sure to go to church. God is bound to notice absentees'. So concluded Selby after she had experienced the spontaneity of Methodist prayer and the juxtaposition of human drama and natural tranquillity in St. Kitts-Nevis. She also advises on places of interest and on the best food to eat on Nevis. The article is illustrated with a picture of a traditional wooden island-house with galvanized iron roof and jalousies.

13 **Penguin guide to the Caribbean.**
   Edited by Alan Tucker. Harmondsworth, England: Penguin, 1991. 301p. maps.
A friendly introduction to St. Kitts-Nevis. The islands, and their major interests, towns and hotels, are vividly described.

14 **St. Kitts: cradle of the Caribbean.**
   Brian Dyde. London: Macmillan, 1989. 120p.
Charmingly illustrated in colour, this is a vivid, general description of St. Kitts. It contains numerous stories about: the fertility of the island; its place as the mother colony of the West Indies; its history as a plantation colony; its emergence from

colony to country; its sugar industry; and its changing economy. Dyde also describes the capital, Basseterre, past and present, the elegant hostelries of the island, and the reputation of St. Kitts as the Gibraltar of the Caribbean.

15 **Statesman's yearbook, 1993-94.**
Edited by John Paxton. London: Macmillan, 1993. 1,710p. maps.

This is a one-volume, annual encyclopaedia with statistical and historical information on every state in the world. Part one deals with international organizations, and part two with countries of the world. Page 1132 deals with St. Kitts and Nevis under the following headings: history, area and population, climate, constitution and government, international relations, economy, energy and natural resources, industry, commerce, tourism, communications, justice, education and welfare, and diplomatic representatives. Separate place, product and person indexes are provided.

16 **A tale of three islands.**
Michael Carlton. *Southern Living*, (March 1991), p. 23-31.

Describes walks through Nevis, which lead visitors to its villages, and to its historical and cultural sites, for example, CocoWalk, Gingerland, Beachlands and Brick Kiln Village, and its centuries-old plantations like the Hermitage Plantation and the Montpelier Estate. Accommodation on Nevis is also listed and illustrations include plantation scenes, the Fig Tree Hill Church, and rowing-boats lazing on the beach. The article also treats Aruba and Puerto Rico.

17 **The world factbook.**
Washington, DC: US Central Intelligence Agency, 1994.

An up-to-date reference source of information on all countries of the world. St. Kitts-Nevis is allocated 3520 words describing: the geography; people and population growth rate; ethnic divisions; religions; languages; literacy; labour force – 20,000 (1981); government; administrative divisions; independence and constitution; legal system; economy; exports and imports; commodities; external debt; industrial production; electricity; industries; agriculture; economic aid; currency; comm-unications; and defence forces.

St. Kitts and Nevis: a tale of two islands.
See item no. 63.

The folklore of St. Christopher's island.
See item no. 144.

St. Kitts and Nevis tourist guide.
See item no. 546.

Geography

General and regional

18 **Geography for C.X.C.**
Wilma Bailey, Patricia H. Pemberton.   Walton-on-Thames, England:
Nelson, 1983. 154p. maps.
This work is aimed at secondary students who are preparing for the Caribbean
Examinations Council (CXC) geography examinations. It deals with topics such as
the physical setting of the Caribbean, sugar, industrialization, transport,
communications, the Caribbean Community (CARICOM) and migration.

19 **The historical geography of St. Kitts and Nevis: the West Indies.**
Gordon Clark Merrill.   Mexico City: Instituto Panamericano de
Geografía e Historia, 1958. 145p. bibliog.
The antecedents and early history of settlement in St. Kitts-Nevis are outlined in this
work, followed by a description of the physical setting of each island. The author
covers the period of Indian occupancy and discusses sugar and slavery as institutions,
and plantations under slavery. Current views on estate and peasant agriculture are
given and general conclusions are drawn. A useful index is provided.

20 **Islands in the sun.**
Basseterre, St. Kitts: Geography Teachers Association, 1986. maps.
bibliog.
A local geography of St. Kitts-Nevis, prepared by educators for use in the islands'
schools. Another interesting and useful work in this field is John Macpherson's
Caribbean Lands (Basingstoke, England: Macmillan, 1963, 200p. maps.). It provides
a detailed account of the geography of St. Kitts-Nevis on p. 117-21, describing
landforms, rainfall, vegetation, agriculture, towns and developments.

21   **A new geography of the Caribbean.**
      Alan Eyre.   London: George Philip & Son, 1962. 162p.
A general survey of the Caribbean region outlining structure, trade and diversity of
population. St. Kitts-Nevis is described as a growing tourist destination, which retains
the old charm of tradition. There are practical exercises and specimen questions
aimed at Comprehensive School pupils, and suggested studies for sixth-formers are
included.

22   **Newton Ground: a farming country.**
      Warren Hanley-Wyatt, Mary Hyligar.   Basseterre, St. Kitts: Ministry
      of Education, Social Studies Committee, 1988. 20p. map. (National
      Heritage Series).
This geographical description of Newton Ground village, St. Kitts, focuses on
location, population, social system, community spirit and occupation.

23   **Touch the happy isles: a journey through the Caribbean.**
      Quentin Crewe.   London: Michael Joseph, 1987. 301p.
Unusual in its approach, this work explores the chain of islands from Trinidad to
Jamaica, tracing the origins of individuality in landscape, history, art and culture. The
author converses with a wide section of the various communities – from fishermen to
prime ministers. Pages 157-84 contain descriptions of the way of life, work and
industries on St. Kitts-Nevis, including agriculture and tourism.

24   **Urbanisation in the Caribbean and trends in global convergence-
      divergence.**
      Robert B. Potter.   *Geographical Journal*, vol. 159, no. 1 (March
      1993), p. 1-21. maps. bibliog.
The polarized pattern of urban settlement during the mercantile and colonial periods
is summarized in this article. According to Potter, the global division of labour for
enclave manufacturing, offshore data processing and tourism is responsible for
contemporary urbanization. Convergence with western norms of consumption, as in
suburbanization, social structuring and aspects of land economy, also adds to the
process of urbanization. Useful illustrations and tables are provided.

25   **The West Indian Islands.**
      George Hunte.   London: Batsford, 1972. 146p. 9 maps. bibliog.
Hunte focuses on the general prehistory and history of the region. He examines the
impact of tourism, arts, crafts, and folklore and the problem of Caribbean identity.

26   **The West Indies.**
      John Quarry.   London: Adam & Black, 1956. 84p. map.
Quarry's aim is 'to give an idea of the curious lands and peoples which make up the
West Indies'. In chapter six, 'The Leeward Islands', St. Kitts is described as the
'battle ground, the oldest British colony, next to Bermuda' (p. 21-23). There is a
reference to Henry Christophe, a Kittitian, who was the last of Haiti's three Negro
leaders, and one of Toussaint's generals in the war against Napoleon's army. The
book is easy to read and serves as a good introduction, especially for teenagers.

The Commonwealth yearbook, 1992.
See item no. 5.

St. Kitts: cradle of the Caribbean.
See item no. 14.

Caribbean migrants: environment and human survival on St. Kitts-Nevis.
See item no. 135.

Caribbean Geography.
See item no. 519.

Geology

27   **The geological history of Mt. Misery volcano, St. Kitts, West Indies.**
P. Baker.   *Overseas Geology and Mineral Resources*, vol.10 (1969),
p. 207-30.
The geological history of the volcano on Mount Misery, renamed Mount Liamuiga in 1983, is provided here, accompained by details and explanations of eruptions. Another article on this topic, 'The geology of Mt. Misery volcano, St. Kitts', can be found in *Fourth Caribbean Geological Conference* ([1965], p. 361-65).

28   **Reports on the geology of the Leeward and British Virgin Islands.**
P. H. A. Martin-Kaye.   Castries, St. Lucia: Voice Publishing, 1959.
117p. maps.
Martin-Kaye gives a detailed analysis of the geology of five countries, namely: Anguilla, Montserrat, Antigua, St. Kitts and the British Virgin Islands. Geological maps and surveys help to clarify the descriptive sections on mineralogy, physical geography, soil sciences and water supplies.

29   **Study of the water resources in Nevis.**
Lemuel E. Pemberton.   Basseterre, St. Kitts: St. Kitts and Nevis
Teachers Training College, 1985. 35p. bibliog.
Studies the extent of the water resources in Nevis under the following headings: physical conditions; present water situation, water resources; progress of projects; and conclusions. Also presented are: a rationale for a teaching unit; the teaching unit; and a lesson plan.

30   **Water sector programme evaluation: Leeward and Windward Islands.**
William L. Sears and Associates.   Ottawa: Canadian International
Development Agency (CIDA), 1983.
Sears reports on the water supply situation in Antigua and Barbuda, Dominica, Grenada, Montserrat, St. Kitts and Nevis, St. Vincent and the Grenadines, and Saint

Lucia. The work relates the reliability of the water supply system to the countries' ability to encourage agricultural development and to attract investment, and makes recommendations in areas including distribution systems, inventory, water storage analysis, automatic storage controls, training and technology selection.

31 **Water supply and sanitation of St. Kitts-Nevis.**
Athill Rawlins.   Basseterre, St. Kitts: St. Kitts-Nevis Government, 1982. 5p.

The organization and administration of water supply are outlined in this short paper, which was presented at the International Water Supply and Sanitation decade: Caribbean and Central American Seminar, in January 1982. Water sources, distribution systems and water quality are described and proposals, including the development of ground water and the installation of short pipelines from reservoirs to areas served, are presented.

32 **Water utility and tariff restructuring study: final report.**
Slaney International.   St. Phillip, Barbados: Government of St. Kitt-Nevis, 1985. 211p.

A very useful document, of particular importance to the Water Department as it provides recommendations for upgrading its management and organizational structure, and for strengthening finances for water supply services. An hydrometric network is recommended, and strong advice is given to Nevis, which has a different surface geology from St. Kitts, to put the conservation of water resources high on its list of priorities.

Climate, hurricanes and disasters

33 **The Christena disaster in retrospect: error, challenge and hope.**
Whitman T. Browne.   Charlotte Amalie, St. Thomas, US Virgin Islands: St. Thomas Graphics, 1985. 141p. maps.

With a foreword by Charles W. Turnbull, Commissioner of Education for the US Virgin Islands, this work relates the story of the *Christena,* a ferry which sank while crossing from St. Kitts to Nevis on 1 August, 1970. Two hundred and forty persons perished, and ninety-one survived. After four years of research, Browne chronicles the details of the sinking, and the consequences of the disaster on individuals and society. The book also deals with the social, political, economical, cultural and religious character of St. Kitts-Nevis and the Caribbean. Appendixes include: List of persons identified; List of persons missing; List of survivors; and Witnesses who gave evidence before the Commission of Inquiry.

34 **Cyclones: Caribbean hurricanes.**
F. C. Farnum.   St. Johns, Antigua: Caribbean Meteorological Institute, 1979. 10p.

An expert hydrometeorologist describes the climatology and related phenomena of Caribbean hurricanes and other natural disasters in the region.

35 **Earthquakes, volcanoes and hurricanes.**
J. Tomblin. *Ambio*, vol. 10, no. 6 (1981).
Tomblin reviews natural hazards and vulnerability in the West Indies.

36 **Eastern Caribbean countries hurricane shelters survey: St. Christopher-Nevis, vol. 2.**
Consulting Engineers Partnership. Basseterre, St. Kitts: Pan American Health Organisation (PAHO), UNDRO, Pan-American disaster preparedness and prevention project (PCPDPPP), 1984. 123p.
This provides a detailed listing of hurricane shelters, each described in terms of its dimensions, general condition and facilities available.

37 **Hurricanes: their nature and history, especially those of the West Indies and the southern coast of the United States.**
Ivan R. Tannehill. Princeton, New Jersey: Princeton University Press, 1938. Reprinted, New York: Greenwood Press, 1969. 157p. maps. bibliog.
Tannehill establishes essential facts about the theories regarding tropical hurricanes in the West Indies and the adjacent waters of the Atlantic Ocean, Gulf of Mexico and Caribbean Sea.

38 **I remember when: the hurricanes of 1924 and 1928.**
Byron R. Spence. *Nevis Historical and Conservation Society Newsletter* (December 1988), p. 14-16.
Recounts the experiences of the 1924 and 1928 hurricanes, noting the differences in the level of preparedness and human relations in the four year span.

39 **Volcanic hazards on St. Kitts and Montserrat, West Indies.**
P. Baker. *Journal of the Geological Society*, vol. 142, no. 2 (1985), p. 279-95. maps.
The history of volcanic activity on both islands is traced. The paper also indicates the location of the volcanic areas and describes the past, current and potential hazards.

40 **Workshop report on disaster preparedness and emergency measures.**
UNDRO. Pan-American disaster preparedness and prevention project, Government of St. Kitts-Nevis. Basseterre, St.Kitts: The Author, 1984. 122p.
Records the proceedings of a workshop which aims to familiarize all levels of government and the public of their roles in the event of a disaster. Participating sectors include: the National Emergency Committee; government and senior statutory boards; officials of voluntary organizations; and other participants.

41   **The world weather guide.**
      E. A. Pearce, C. G. Smith.   London: Hutchinson, 1984. 480p. bibliog.

An excellent work which describes the weather that can be expected in any part of the world at any given time during the year. The Caribbean is dealt with on pages 315-29. Tables for the islands' weather stations and monthly details of temperature, humidity and precipitation are provided.

Maps and atlases

42   **Macmillan Caribbean certificate atlas.**
      London: Macmillan, 1978. 2nd ed. 104p. maps.

The atlas includes maps of the region's physical and political geography and tropical disturbances.

43   **Nevis: preliminary data atlas.**
      Eastern Caribbean Natural Area Management Programme.   In: *Survey of conservation priorities in the Lesser Antilles, 26 vols.*   Eastern Caribbean Natural Area Management.   Ann Arbor, Michigan: University of Michigan, Caribbean Conservation Association, 1980. 21p. maps.

Data in this atlas refers particularly to Nevis, and indicates where nature conservation is concentrated. It also pinpoints: population density; resources conservation; endangered species; national parks; and nature reserves.

44   **St. Kitts and Nevis.**
      London: Ministry of Overseas Development (Directorate of Overseas Surveys), 1 sheet.

A large, colour map of St. Kitts, showing land features, vegetation, roads, hotels, airports, post offices, drawn on a scale of 1:25,000. There is also a separate, similar map for Nevis. The maps are available from the Ordinance Survey, Romsey Road, Southampton, England SO9 4DH and also from the Survey Department in St. Kitts-Nevis.

45   **St. Kitts: preliminary data atlas.**
      Eastern Caribbean Natural Area Management Programme.   In: *Survey of conservation priorities in the Lesser Antilles, 26 vols.*   Eastern Caribbean Natural Area Management.   Ann Arbor, Michigan: University of Michigan, Caribbean Conservation Association, 1980. 21p. maps.

Data in this atlas shows where nature conservation is concentrated and indicates population density, resources conservation, endangered species, national parks, and nature reserves. Land use methods are also defined. The meeting of the Natural Area Management Programme was held in Christiansted, St. Croix.

46   **Wall map of the Caribbean.**
    Basingstoke, England: Macmillan, [n.d].
The map, 850 x 1,220 mm with a scale of 1:3,500,00, was produced in association
with the West Indian Committee. It covers basic aspects of regional geography, and
indicates sea routes and CARICOM membership. St. Kitts-Nevis is included.

Historic heritage of St. Kitts, Nevis, Anguilla.
See item no. 105.

Island environments and development.
See item no. 362.

Nevis resource assessment and zoning plan.
See item no. 363.

St. Kitts-Nevis country environmental profile.
See item no. 364.

The Southeast Peninsular project in St. Kitts.
See item no. 365.

Town and country planning in St. Kitts-Nevis.
See item no. 366.

**Land use management plan for the Southeast Peninsular of St. Kitts, West
Indies.**
See item no. 381.

Sailing and cruising guides

47   **A cruising guide to the Lesser Antilles.**
    Donald Street.   Boston, Massachusetts: Sail Books, 1994. 320p. maps.
Provides excellent coverage of and guidance to the area, offering: general yachting
information; descriptions of harbours and anchorages; entry and communications;
navigational aids; and sailing directories. Specific information on St. Kitts-Nevis
appears throughout the work, for example on p. 148-55 where St. Kitts-Nevis is noted
as being 'the last refuge for sailing lighters in the Antilles'. The advantages and
disadvantages of several anchorages are given. Street has also written *The ocean
sailing yacht* (New York: W. W. Norton & Co. Ltd., 1973 [vol. 1], 1979 [vol. 2]) and
regularly contributes to *Sail Magazine.*

48   **Divers delight: St. Kitts and Saba aboard the Caribbean Explorer.**
    Michael Lawrence.   *Skin Diver*, vol. 40 (October 1991), p. 70-76.
Lawrence describes in detail this live-aboard boat, which offers such amenities as
access to superior diving locations, comfort and a competent staff. Excursions are
available to some of St. Kitts' outstanding beaches.

Travellers' Accounts

Pre-20th century

49 **Familiar letters to Henry Clay of Kentucky describing a winter in the West Indies.**
J. J. Gurney.   New York: Mahlon Day & Co., 1840. 203p.
This account mocks the chilly winters of the Americas and seems intent upon charming away its citizens to resettle in the Caribbean.

50 **A voyage in the West Indies: containing various observations made during a residence in Barbados and several of the Leeward Islands; with some notices and illustrations relative to the city of Paramaribo in Surinam.**
John Augustine Waller.   London: printed for Sir Richard Phillips & Co., Bridge Court, Bridge Street, 1820. 106p. map.
Waller recounts his experience in the West Indies, paying much attention to scenic and geographical details and the weather situation.

51 **A voyage to the islands of Madera, Barbados, Nieves, S. Christopher and Jamaica, with the natural history of the herbs and trees, four-footed beasts, fishes, birds, insects, reptiles etc.**
Sir H. Sloane.   London: printed by B.M. for the author, 1725. 2 vols.
This early account in two volumes with several maps and illustrations, gives a detailed description of the Caribbean of a bygone age. St. Kitts is given special attention as England's first colony in the Caribbean. It covers the period 1707-25.

52   **West India sketch book.**
    London: Whitaker & Co., 1834. A reprint.
Records a miscellany of facts and figures which give an economic and social insight
into the state of the West Indies in the 17th and 18th centuries.

20th-century description and travel

53   **Charlestown, Nevis.**
    Riva Berleant-Schiller, Arnold Berleant.   *Focus*, (Fall, 1978),
    p. 32-33.
Presents Charlestown, the capital of Nevis. This miniature port is an historic West
Indian town with most of its architecture intact and its configuration of streets and
walkways largely unaltered, despite three centuries of economic and social change.
Both official and domestic architecture is described in some detail and the
illustrations, namely, Charlestown street framed by Nevis Peak, and Walwyn Plaza
fronted by graceful British colonial buildings, add much interest to this article.

54   **Coasting in the Caribbean – Lesser Antilles.**
    Nicholas Crane.   *World Magazine,* (August 1991), p. 28-33.
The author's tour of the islands by bicycle is described here, with some space devoted
to a trip around Nevis.

55   **The life of the landed gentry.**
    E. D. Smith.   *Black Enterprise* (May 1986), p. 79-88.
Describes the daily life-style of the twin-nation of St. Kitts and Nevis, with details of
the town centre, restaurants, historical and plantation sites on p. 74 and 83. The article
appears in the section entitled 'The secret life of the Caribbean'.

56   **The perfect little undiscovered island.**
    Ian Keown.   *Metropolitan Home*, (December 1983), p. 93-98, 121.
Having written this book a few months after independence from Britain, the author
prophesies that Nevis is unlikely to change, giving several reasons for this claim. He
also provides a brief historical sketch and descriptions of several plantation houses,
including Nisbet Plantation Inn, Montpelier Plantation Inn, Crony's Old Manor
Estate, Golden Rock Estate and Zetland Plantation. Ian Keown is also the author of
five guidebooks, including *Caribbean hideaways* (New York: Crown Pubs. Inc.,
1988) and *Very special places.*

Tourism

Guides and information

57 Bequia, Dominica, St. Kitts, Tobago.
Ian Keown, Martin Rapp. *Travel and Leisure*, vol. 22 (January 1992), p. 80-90.
Describes tourist development on each of the islands mentioned in the title, including St. Kitts, where resorts are being built on the beaches. Travel, accommodation and attractions are also listed.

58 The Caribbean, Bermuda and the Bahamas 1991.
Stephen Birnbaum, Alexander Birnbaum. Boston, Massachusetts: Houghton Mifflin, 1990. 974p. maps.
A general guide which provides glimpses of places of historical and cultural interest on each island in the region. It also directs readers to other sources of information about the best hotels.

59 Caribbean explorer.
Doug Perrine. *Skin Diver*, (August 1990), p. 104-71.
Perrine describes an extraordinary dive/cruise to St. Martin, Saba and St. Kitts. He offers a glimpse into St. Kitts' underwater world museum: 'giant coral encrusted anchors and other relics in the water off the base of Brimstone Hill where British cannon balls found the ships of the French invaders who captured the fort briefly in 1782.' Other sites worthy of a visit are the wrecks *River Taw* and *Talata*, and the Monkey Shoals, a gently sloping reef between St. Kitts and Nevis.

60 **Follow the sun.**
   Chris Core. *Washingtonian*, vol. 27 (December 1991), p. 138-39.
   Describes the Four Seasons resort, built on 350 acres on and above one of Nevis' best beaches. Golf is the resort's primary attraction, but a variety of other activities are offered.

61 **The official St. Kitts-Nevis tourist guide.**
   St. Johns, Antigua: Financial Times Caribbean, 1989. maps.
   An excellent guidebook for the tourist, which offers general information on the country, and suggestions of things to do, such as shopping, guides, tours, and experiencing the local cuisine. The section on history and legends makes fascinating reading. Another interesting introduction to St. Kitts-Nevis is Marcia Kelly's article 'Islands in the sun', which appeared in *St. Paul Magazine* (November 1983, p. 151–61). Kelly describes everyday life on the islands and the work of the local artisans, concluding that the nation's economy will come to depend more and more on tourism.

62 **Pocket guide to the West Indies.**
   Algernon Aspinall. London: Methuen, 1954. 474p. maps.
   A popular guide giving a general introduction to the West Indies, and including information on political and economic changes, educational facilities, security and industries. St. Kitts is described in Chapter eight on p. 225-35 and Nevis on p. 226-42. Interesting historical sites are described with occasional quotations from earlier travellers. Originally published in 1907, revised in 1954 by J. Sydney Dash, and reprinted in 1960, this work is a classic guide, enhanced by thirty-two maps and twenty-five plates.

63 **St. Kitts and Nevis: a tale of two islands.**
   Helmut Koenig, Gea Koenig. *Travel Holiday*, (Febuary 1981), p. 62-74.
   There is a classic curve of development as island resorts move from obscurity into the spotlight, which can bring about a gradual decline of interest. However, according to Helmut and Gea Koenig, St. Kitts and Nevis are managing to hold on to their special qualities, features which were thought to have gone out of style. The article is profusely illustrated, and includes the inscriptions and drawings of Carib Indians on rocks.

Social and economic impact

64 **Is tourism a potential engine of growth?**
   Neville Nicholls. In: *Statements of the President delivered at annual meetings of Board of Governors, 1980-89.* Bridgetown, Barbados: Caribbean Development Bank, 1988, p. 177-86.
   At a meeting held in St. Kitts on 9-10 May 1988, Nicholls presents the case for the benefits of tourism to the Caribbean generally and to specific islands, with some comment on the effects on St. Kitts-Nevis.

65 **Optimum size and nature of new hotel development in the Caribbean.**
Executive Secretariat for Economic and Social Affairs. Washington, DC: Dept. of Regional Development, Organisation of American States, 1987. 49p. maps.

St. Kitts-Nevis is covered in this general work dealing with: tourism development and its requirements; the hotel industry; and the need to regulate its growth. Another relevant publication on this topic is: 'Tourism investment and ownership: local versus foreign', by Simon Jones-Hendrickson (*Bulletin of Eastern Caribbean Affairs*, vol. 8, no. 5 [1982], p. 31-36).

66 **St. Kitts-Nevis tourism master plan.**
Edited by Mark Mercready. Washington, DC: Executive Secretariat for Economic and Social Affairs, Organisation of American States, 1993. 103p. maps. bibliog.

A work of much depth and importance, describing existing tourism in St. Kitts-Nevis, and giving the context of planning for tourism development. It also describes national goals, the physical plan, the marketing plan, institutional needs, human resources development, public sector projects and programmes. Methods of financing the activities of the plan are proposed, and numerous tables, in set maps, figures and appendixes assist in clarifying these proposals. The appendixes include inventories of: natural attractions; hotels, guest houses, villas and apartments; and tours. Architectural guidelines for tourism development and project profiles are included. The project was coordinated by Maria E. Bacci.

67 **The social impact of tourism in Nevis.**
Colin Tyrell. *Nevis Historical and Conservation Society Newsletter*, vol. 16 (June 1989), p. 10-11.

Tourism can have a positive effect in Nevis, both socially and economically, if the Government plans appropriately and implements clear policies, according to Tyrell. Factors such as social interaction, increased economic activity, land use, gambling and prostitution, drugs and psychological pressures all have an impact upon the social well-being of the island and its people. Therefore, in an island as small as Nevis, tourism must be considered in its proper perspective. Samuel Caines also contributes an article under the title 'Economic impact of tourism on Nevis' in the same volume of the *Newsletter*, p. 8-9.

68 **Some aspects of the possible effects of tourism on agricultural development in the States of St. Kitts-Nevis-Anguilla.**
K. Archibald. *Proceedings, Wisconsin Agriculture and Economics Centre*, vol. 5 (1970), p. 34-39.

Archibald expresses traditional, professional, scientific and cultural concerns for the development of agriculture, in terms of the country's ability to accommodate the additional needs of tourism.

69   **Tourism and the environment.**
Nevis Historical and Conservation Society. *Nevis Historical and Conservation Society Newsletter*, vol. 16 (June 1989), p. 12-13.
Escalated tourism development is triggering environmental problems in Nevis, according to this article. These problems include: sand mining; silt and debris (from building too close to the sea) washing into it killing corals and seagrass beds; waste from cruise ships, cargo vessels and yachts; maintenance of historic sites; and endangered species. The recommendation is for cautious and timely planning which puts the environment and islanders first: this is necessary in order to develop an environmentally friendly tourism industry and to nurture both the natural beauty and the identity of Nevis.

70   **Tourism: arrivals up in St. Kitts-Nevis.**
Research and Statistics.   Basseterre, St. Kitts: Ministry of Tourism, 1994.
According to this report from the Manager of Research and Statistics at the Ministry of Tourism, St. Kitts and Nevis has recorded a 16.3 per cent increase in long-stay tourist arrivals, for the first quarter of 1994. A break-down of the 29,586 visitors into nationals of America, Canada, the United Kingdom, Europe and the Organisation of Eastern Caribbean States (OECS) is provided. Revenue from tourists in this quarter totalled EC $78 million.

Annual digest of statistics for 1982.
See item no. 254.

Caribbean Tourism Statistical Report.
See item no. 255.

Statistical digest 1989: Nevis.
See item no. 257.

Integration of agriculture and tourism.
See item no. 298.

Caribbean Tourism.
See item no. 526.

St. Kitts and Nevis Quarterly Tourism Bulletin.
See item no. 545.

Flora and Fauna

General

71   **Flora and fauna of the Caribbean.**
Peter R. Bacon.   Port of Spain, Trinidad: Key Caribbean Publications,
1978. 319p. map.

This is a general introduction to the ecology of the Caribbean area. It takes the form
of an ecological tour, covering: Caribbean rain forests; coral reefs; sand beaches;
rocky shores; mangrove swamps; rivers; savannas; caves; desert islands; and man-
made environments. There are over 200 line drawings and photographs, plus 32 full
colour plates. The general background and ecological principles apply to the entire
area. Reference is made to St. Kitts-Nevis and the arrival of the green monkey, C.
sabaeus, during the 18th century, on p. 289. The work is aimed at naturalists and
students and anyone who wishes to understand the relationships of life in the natural
environment.

72   **The islands of the sea.**
John Murray.   London: Oxford University Press, 1991. 329p. bibliog.

The editor presents five centuries of nature writing in the Caribbean under intriguing
titles such as: Paradise found – age of conquest; paradise lost – age of colonisation;
paradise recalled – age of conscience, etc. There is an informed essay which gives an
overview of the literature on the islands, and a comprehensive index enhances the use
of this historical and contemporary work.

73   **A natural history of Nevis and the rest of the English Leeward**
      Caribee Islands in America with many other observations on
      nature and art, particularly an introduction to the art of
      decyphering.
William Smith.   Cambridge, England: J. Bentham, 1745. 327p.

Describes the animal and plant life in the islands, paying particular attention to Nevis.

Flora

74 **Cactus studies in the West Indies.**
N. L. Britton. *Journal of the New York Botanical Garden*, vol. 14, no. 161 (1913), p. 99.
In this general article on cacti of the region, there are several references to species found on St. Kitts.

75 **Caribbean flora.**
C. D. Adams. Walton-on-Thames, England: Thomas Nelson, 1976. 63p.
A study of selected Caribbean flowers and plants, giving their classification, structure, physiology and economic importance. Lavishly illustrated, it serves as a useful comparison with other standard works.

76 **Flora of the Lesser Antilles: Orchideae.**
Leslie A. Garey, Herman R. Sweet. New York: Arnold Arboretum, Harvard University, 1974.
An impressive and authoritative work on the orchids of the Lesser Antillian islands. The distribution of each orchid species is defined and recorded, based on first-hand information and herbaria. According to Garey and Sweet, there are 129 species in the entire Lesser Antilles and only four species have been found on Nevis.

77 **Sex, games and the orchids of Nevis.**
Thomas Huggins. *Nevis Historical and Conservation Society Newsletter*, no. 32 (November 1993), p. 4-6.
Huggins presents a realistic estimate of Nevisian orchid diversity based on his latest collections made during ten weeks in 1992 and 1993. He found twenty-two species (listed in the work) naturally occurring in Nevis and proposes that the species diversity of other nearby islands, like St. Kitts and Montserrat, is also much higher than is generally accepted. The article is well illustrated and documented.

78 **A survey of the dominant flora in three wetlands habitats on Nevis, West Indies.**
D. Rodrigues. St. Laurent, Canada: Vanier College Press, 1990.
This is a description of the actual survey of three wetland habitats in Nevis, and forms the basis of another work by the author entitled 'Dominant flora and vegetation zones of Nevis', completed in the same year.

79 **Tropical blossoms.**
Dorothy Hargreaves, Bob Hargreaves. Oregon: Hargreaves Industrial, [n.d.]. 48p.
This is a handy guide to the botany of selected flowering plants found in most Caribbean islands, with full-page colour illustrations. Another recent publication of interest is 'Gardening in the Caribbean' by Iris Bannochie and Marilyn Light.

Bannochie established the Angromeda Gardens in Barbados, and won several prizes including three gold medals for entries at the Chelsea Flower Show in London. The book is illustrated in colour with much practical information about gardening.

Fauna

80 The birds of St. Kitts-Nevis.
S. Danforth. *Tropical Agriculture*, vol. 10 (1936), p. 213-17.

An illustrated description of the birds of St. Kitts-Nevis, giving name, class and habitat. Another publication providing informed discussion and raising various concerns is *The effects of development on the avi-fauna of St. Kitts* by M. Morris and R. Lemon (Montreal: McGill University, Biological Dept., 1982).

81 Birds of the West Indies.
James Bond. Boston, Massachusetts: Houghton Mifflin, 1986. 5th American ed. 256p. maps.

Several references are made to St. Kitts-Nevis bird locations in Bond's classic guide to Caribbean birds. It gives classification, characteristics and habitats of the birds to be found in the Caribbean region.

82 Butterflies and other insects of the Eastern Caribbean.
P. D. Stiling. London: Macmillan, 1986. 85p.

Using clear and bold illustrations, Stiling guides the beginner progressively through the entomology of the region.

83 Guide to corals and fishes of Florida, the Bahamas and the Caribbean.
Idaz Greenberg. Miami, Florida: Seahawk Press, 1977. 64p.

A general, handy reference to 260 species of corals and fishes, illustrated in full colour. It gives the local and scientific names of each species, their chief characteristics and their length. An index further enhances the volume's usefulness.

84 Island lists of West Indian amphibians and reptiles.
W. Maclean. Washington, DC: Smithsonian Herpetological Service, 1977. (No. 40).

Provides students and enthusiastic environmentalists with a useful checklist of amphibians and reptiles in the area.

85   **The living reef: corals and fishes of Florida, the Bahamas, Bermuda and the Caribbean.**
Jerry Greenberg, Idaz Greenberg.   Miami, Florida: Seahawk Press, 1972. 110p.

A lavishly-illustrated guide with large, colour photographs. The formation of coral reefs is explained, and the index to both common and scientific names of corals and fishes will make this book popular with young marine enthusiasts.

86   **The St. Kitts green monkey.**
F. Poirier.   *Folia Primatologica*, vol. 17 (1972), p. 20-25.

Poirier presents the ecology, population dynamics and selected behavioural traits of the St. Kitts green monkey (*Cercopithecus aethiops sabaeus*).

87   **The St. Kitts vervet.**
M. McGuire.   *Contributions to Primatology*, vol. 1 (1974). maps.

This entire volume, with its twelve figures, thirteen tables and fourteen maps, is dedicated to the St. Kitts vervet. Another interesting publication is 'Vervet monkey troupe movements and activity patterns for Golden Rock Estates, Nevis' by J. Bermingham (St. Laurent, Quebec: Vanier College Press, 1990).

Caribbean islands handbook.
See item no. 3.

The dancing sisters.
See item no. 6.

Afro Caribbean folk medicine: the reproduction and practice of healing.
See item no. 176.

Edible fruits and vegetables of the English-speaking Caribbean.
See item no. 315.

The Southeast Peninsular project in St. Kitts.
See item no. 365.

Agronomy Monthly Report.
See item no. 512.

Caribbean Conservation News.
See item no. 515.

Nevis Historical and Conservation Society Newsletter.
See item no. 537.

St. Christopher Society Heritage Magazine.
See item no. 541.

Prehistory and Archaeology

88   Aboriginal antiquities of St. Kitts-Nevis.

C. W. Branch.   *American Anthropologica*, vol. 9, no. 2 (April-June 1907), p. 325-33.

In this expertly illustrated article, Branch describes: pottery art from the remains found in an Indian grave; petroglyphs at four locations; middens of six Indian settlements in St. Kitts and two in Nevis; and mortuary remains. He makes interesting comments on each of the above areas, especially on the way that ornamentation is achieved on the pottery. There are appropriate illustrations, for example: fig. 25, Sections of lips of pottery vessels; fig. 26, Incised patterns on pottery; fig. 27, Fragment of human mask in pottery; and fig. 28. Turtle's head in pottery.

89   An archaeological reconnaissance of St. Kitts, Leeward Islands.

L. Allaire.   In: *Proceedings of the fifth international congress for the study of the pre-Columbian cultures of the Lesser Antilles.*   Tempe, Arizona: Arizona State University, 1974, p. 158-61.

The findings of an archaeological expedition on St. Kitts are reported.

90   On the trail of the Arawaks.

Fred Olsen, foreword by George Kubler, introductory essay by Irving Rouse.   Norman, Oklahoma: University of Oklahoma Press, 1974. 408p. maps. bibliog.

This work relates the story of the author's search for the origins of the first Indians encountered by Christopher Columbus on his voyages to the New World. Olsen explains how his team discovered the Arawaks, and he expounds their religion, petroglyphs, culture and games. He traces their origins as evidenced in an eight-page section of colour photographs describing Arawak sites and sculpture. There are also many illustrations showing sherds, bowls, tools, *zemis* (Indian god) and petroglyphs found throughout the Lesser Antilles, especially in Antigua. This is a very important work on the archaeology of the entire region.

91 **Papers in Caribbean anthropology.**
Edited by Irving Rouse, compiled by Sidney Mintz. New Haven,
Connecticut: Yale University, Department of Anthropology, 1970. 252p.
bibliog. (Yale University Publications in Anthropology, nos. 57-64).
Eight papers which deal with some of the sociological, economical, archaeological
and ethnological problems of the Caribbean. The article entitled 'The entry of man
into the West Indies' by Rouse, which questions how and from where the aboriginal
homo caribensis arrived in the islands, makes stimulating reading.

92 **Shellfish gatherers of St. Kitts.**
D. Armstrong. In: *Proceedings of the eighth international congress
for the study of the pre-Columbian cultures of the Lesser Antilles.*
Edited by S. Lewenstein. Tempe, Arizona: Arizona State University,
1980, p. 152-67.
A study of the archaic subsistence and settlement patterns in St. Kitts.

93 **The Tainos: the rise and decline of the people who greeted
Columbus.**
Irving Rouse. New Haven, Connecticut: Yale University Press, 1992.
232p.
An interesting account of the spread of the Tainos through the Caribbean, including
St. Kitts-Nevis, until the time of the arrival of the Europeans.

94 **Wild majesty: encounters with the Caribs from Columbus to the
present day.**
Edited by Peter Hulme, Neil Whitehead. London: Oxford University
Press, 1992. 369p. maps.
This anthology of European encounters with Amerindians in the Caribbean enlightens
many issues of 'culture contacts and the growth of imperial attitudes'. Source
material such as the reports of Columbus, missionary writings, travellers' stories,
colonial administrative reports, ethnographic writing and others, are used to give a
fascinating account of perceptions on the one hand, and acculturation on the other.
There is a map of the Lesser Antilles with their native names; for instance, Nevis was
'Qualiti' and St. Kitts, 'Liamuiga'. Other references appear as follows: St. Kitts on
p. 52-3; 89; 94-6; 100; 103-05; 109-10; and Nevis on p. 29; 35; 95; 101; 104.

St. Kitts and Nevis: a tale of two islands.
See item no. 63.

From Columbus to Castro: history of the Caribbean 1492-1969.
See item no. 102.

Caribbean Conservation News.
See item no. 515.

Journal of Caribbean Studies.
See item no. 534.

Prehistory and Archaeology

Nevis Historical and Conservation Society Newsletter.
See item no. 537.

St. Christopher Society Heritage Magazine.
See item no. 541.

History

General and regional

95 **Afro-Caribbean villages in historical perspective.**
Edited by Charles V. Carnegie.   Kingston, Jamaica: African Caribbean
Institute, 1987. 133p.

The historical development of particular Caribbean communities is the central theme
of this book. It brings together several case-studies which provide an invaluable
methodological tool, opening up to scrutiny the history and organization of village
communities in the Caribbean. Contributors Sidney W. Mintz, Karen Fog Olwig,
Trevor Purcell, O. Nigel Bollard, Charles V. Carnegie and Jean Besson share a
common concern: to understand African cultural continuities within the dynamic social
context of the Caribbean communities in which they took on new life and significance.

96 **An attempt at planned settlement in St. Kitts, in the early
eighteenth century.**
D. L. Niddrie.   *Caribbean Studies*, vol. 5, no. 4 (1966), p. 3-11.

Niddrie contrasts the highly sophisticated Spanish system of colonization and land
development in the Caribbean with the haphazard colonizing expeditions of the
English. He describes the French invasion and the general devastation inflicted on St.
Kitts, and the start of the importation of Negro slaves, which created the traditional
West Indian plantation society of the 18th century.

97 **Caribbeana.**
V. L. Oliver.   London: Mitchell, Hughes & Clark, 1910-1919. 6 vols.

Extracts from St. Kitts-Nevis' wills of 1629, bequests of sugar, land and slaves, and
other documents make up this collection of miscellaneous papers, relating to the
history, genealogy, topography and antiquities of the British West Indies. They
provide an invaluable insight into the scenes of yesteryear.

98 **Caribbean islands under the proprietary patents.**
James A. Wiliamson. London: Oxford University Press, 1926. 234p.
maps.
Williamson outlines the origin of proprietary patents, after giving an account of the
colonization of the Caribbean. A description of the first settlement on St. Kitts can be
found on p. 21. The following topics are discussed in detail: the establishment of
government; the administration of the first Earl of Carlisle; the loss of proprietary
rights; the decay of proprietary authority; the interregnum; the Pembroke patent; and the
restoration settlement. There are ten references to St. Kitts and eight to Nevis; those
dealing with colonization are on p. 22-32 and those with regard to partition on p. 71-74.

99 **The case of the present possessors of the French lands in the island
of St. Christopher.**
London: St. Christopher (Official), 1721. 22p.
The case is humbly offered to the consideration of his Majesty and to both houses of
parliament.

100 **The conqueror: being the true and romantic story of Alexander
Hamilton.**
Gertrude F. Atherton. London, New York: Macmillan, 1902. 546p.
An historical novel about the lawyer and statesman, Alexander Hamilton (1757-
1804), which Atherton bases on the Hamilton family papers and public records in the
West Indies. It tells of Hamilton's youth in the West Indies and in the colonies of
North America.

101 **The French invasion of St. Kitts-Nevis.**
Thomas Reginald St. Johnson. Basseterre, St. Kitts: Society for the
Restoration of Brimstone Hill, 1970. 20p. map.
With the illustrative assistance of four leaves of plates, the author ably describes the
dramatic and turbulent period in the history of St. Kitts-Nevis, when the French army
invaded.

102 **From Columbus to Castro: the history of the Caribbean 1492-
1969.**
Eric Williams. London: André Deutsch, 1970. 576p. maps. bibliog.
All aspects of Caribbean history are dealt with in this general history of the region.
There are forty-four references to St. Kitts-Nevis, from p. 79-498.

103 **A handbook of St. Kitts-Nevis.**
Katherine J. Burdon. London: The West India Committee, 1920.
247p. maps.
A useful source for the study of St. Kitts-Nevis-Anguilla's colonial past and
administration. Part one describes the general presidency in two chapters, covering
constitution and statistics. Part two deals with St. Kitts in fifteen chapters which
discuss the following topics: history; health and hospitals; agriculture; geology; flora
and fauna; education; postal and other communication matter; miscellaneous
administrative details; list of estates; institutions; information for tourists; and

excursions. Part three treats Nevis in chapters 16-27, and part four describes Anguilla in chapters 28-34. There are numerous photographs and other illustrations of civic and historic buildings and places.

104 Historic Basseterre: the story of a West Indian town.
Probyn Inniss. Basseterre, St. Kitts: The author, 1985. 84p. maps. bibliog.

This illustrated work is a rich source of comparison between old Basseterre and other historical West Indian towns. The author describes Basseterre: during the French occupation; from 1713-1838; and from 1838 to the present. Individual topics covered are: health facilities; churches and schools; disasters; the growth of commerce; the government; public buildings, monuments and utilities; and cultural and recreational facilities.

105 Historic heritage of St. Kitts, Nevis, Anguilla.
Kathleen D. Manchester, foreword by A. L. Lam. Port of Spain, Trinidad: Syncreators Ltd, 1971. 138p. maps.

A comprehensive treatment of the subject. Topics are discussed in great detail, and include: historical sites; metropolitan policies and local rivalries; churches and religion; intellectual, literary and debating interests; natural disasters; milestones in education; old harbours; the march of time and modern Basseterre; famous personalities; music, dance and drama; arts and crafts; sports; community activities; and loyalty to royalty. It covers the period from the 17th century to the present day and includes historical photographs and maps.

106 The historical background of the British Empire in the Caribbean.
Bryan Edwards. London: John Stockdale, 1801. 3 vols.

Several other versions of the original work have been published in the years as follows: 1793; 1798; 1807; and 1966.

107 History of the British West Indies.
Alan Burns. London: Allen & Unwin, 1954. 2nd rev. ed. 1965. 849p. maps. bibliog.

A comprehensive account of the history of the West Indies, also including detailed descriptions of countries outside the 'British Empire'. Another relevant title, with references to St. Kitts-Nevis on p. 15, is *Europe in the Caribbean*, edited by Paul Sutton (London, Basingstoke: Macmillan Caribbean, 1991. 260p).

108 The history of St. Christopher.
John Oldmixon. In: *The British Empire in America*, vol.2. London: printed for John Nicholson at King's Arms in Little Britain, Benjamin Tooke at the Middle Temple Gate, Fleet Street, and Richard Parker and Ralph Smith under the Piazza of The Royal Exchange, 1708, p. 220-62.

Contains an account of the discovery and settlement of St. Kitts, which treats the climate, soil, products and trade, events and inhabitants of the island. There is a similar account on Nevis in the same volume on p. 195-219.

109 **Precis of information concerning the Presidency of Saint Christopher.**
Basseterre, St. Kitts: St. Christopher – Official, 1877. 81p.
This work is of much historical significance. It describes the country's geography and topography; harbours, roadsteads and landing places; communications – roads and tracks; railways; rivers and canals; telegraphs and steamers; towns and settlements; forts, arsenals, stores, barracks and means of sheltering troops; dockyards and naval establishments; climate as it affects products and health; trade, agriculture, productions; inhabitants – character, pursuits and languages; history; internal administration; finance; moneys, weights and measures; and the army and navy.

110 **The real Alexander Hamilton was a Black man!**
Abiola Sinclair. *The Ethnic News Watch*, vol. 84, no. 14 (3 April 1993), p. 26.
Sinclair traces Alexander Hamilton's roots to the Leeward Island of Nevis where he was born, in 1757, to Rachel Faucette, 'a Black woman, proud and intelligent whose father was a French doctor'. Alexander's father, James Hamilton, a Scot, was an unsuccessful planter. Using the biographical and eyewitness accounts of Maclean and others, e.g. Colonel Pickering, Sinclair describes Alexander's relationships with his mother, father, and brother, and his education in the USA, which was paid for by his mother and her family. The article explains the pros and cons of passing for white at that time and cites surveys which indicate that: in 1929, 5,000 Blacks each year crossed over and became 'White'; in 1950 the number was 12,000; and by 1980 it was 17,000. Sinclair speaks of Hamilton's rise to fame as advisor to George Washington and as a major-general in the Continental Army. He was also the founder of the Republican Party, and author of many of the Federalist Papers (documents establishing the thirteen colonies into a federation), and first requested that Black troops be allowed in the Revolutionary Army.

111 **Two hundred years on: the war of American Independence and the independence of St. Kitts and Nevis.**
Graham Norton. *Round Table*, no. 287 (1983), p. 317-27.
Norton describes how, when the American War of Independence came to an end in 1783, the islands of St. Kitts and Nevis, which had been in French hands, came once again under the sovereignty of the British, who had first colonized the islands in 1623. However, the subsequent centuries saw a shift in the relationship between the colonizing force and the colonized, explained thus by the author: 'The difficulties of the trading system and the economic decline of the plantations diminished the role of Britain in the Caribbean as an economic force, and drew the islands into trade with the USA, reforging a link of 200 years ago'.

112 **Whither bound – St. Kitts-Nevis?**
Probyn Inniss. Basseterre, St. Kitts: the author, 1983. 99p. map.
A concise history of St. Kitts-Nevis, from the period of colonization to the present day. The constitutional and political evolution of each island are detailed, with particular focus on the relationship and the historical rivalry between them. The final chapter poses the question 'whither bound?', and concludes that the future depends on two issues: how long the federation of St. Kitts-Nevis lasts; and how soon the 'politics of vengeance' gripping St. Kitts will end. Another useful publication is *Caribbean*

certificate history: Bk 3, Development and decolonisation, by R. Greenwood and S. Hamber (London, Basingstoke: Macmillan Educational, 1981. 182p.).

Slavery and emancipation

113 **Caribbean slave society and economy: a student reader.**
Edited by Hilary Beckles, Verene Shepherd. Kingston, Jamaica: Ian Randle Publishers, 1991. 480p.

The historical writings brought together in this work deal with the entire Caribbean slave society and economy for the duration of slavery in the area. It covers: the decline of the Amerindian people; the establishment of the African slave trade in the area; and the abolition of slavery. Arranged in ten sections, it includes headings such as: 'Production, profitability and markets'; 'Caribbean slavery and the capitalist world economy'; 'Health, nutrition and the crisis of social reproduction'; and 'Slave women, family and households'. The excerpts provide a useful reference to important themes which have appeared in the volume of Caribbean books produced over several decades. The editors, both Caribbean historians, explore topical and modern themes keenly and imaginatively.

114 **Free coloureds in the slave societies of St. Kitts and Grenada, 1763-1833.**
Edward Locksley Cox. Knoxville, Tennessee: University of Tennessee Press, 1984. 197p. bibliog.

With the exception of chapter five, which deals exclusively with revolutions on Grenada, 1795-96, this book pays much attention to St. Kitts. It deals with: demographic patterns; the transition from slavery to freedom; free coloureds in the economy; civil rights; religion and education; the New World perspective; and assessment and evaluation. The work speaks of 'revolutionary change, although hesitantly, during the 1820s as a result of free coloured demands and the waning power of the planter class in both territories'. There are charts, tables, an index and prolific notes.

115 **Slave populations of the British Caribbean 1807-1934.**
B. W. Higman. Baltimore, Maryland: Johns Hopkins University Press, 1984. 781p. maps. bibliog.

The twelve chapters of this work deal successively with: slavery and comparative history; materials and methods; physical and economic environments; growth and distribution of slave populations; the structure of slave populations; urban regimes; health; fertility; morality and natural increase; refuse and resistance; slavery and population history; and statistical material. Numerous appendixes include notes, an index, a list of figures, graphs and tables, which increase the value of the work to users. A map on page xxix shows the parishes and divisions of St. Kitts.

116 **The slavery of the British West India Islands.**
James Stephen. London: J. Butterworth & Son, 1824. Reprinted,
New York: Kraus, 1969. 2 vols.

Volume one of Stephen's work deals with the laws relating to slavery in the islands; volume two looks at the actual practice of slavery, i.e, management, the treatment of slaves, etc. Another work, *Black people in the British Empire: an introduction*, by P. Fryer (London: Pluto Press, 1988. 174p.), describes St. Kitts-Nevis' resistance to apprenticeship on p. 95-96.

Plantations

117 **Essex and sugar.**
Frank Lewis. Chichester, England; London: Phillimore, 1976. 132p.
bibliog.

Lewis' interest in both Essex and sugar inspired him to search for historical and other connections between them. The result is a well-researched and documented, scholarly work, which is superbly illustrated, and is packed with historical detail. The work traces the sources of sugar to Essex and the chapters pertaining to the West Indies, chapters three to six, are entitled: 'Cane sugar 1700-1860'; 'Essex Admirals and the sugar islands'; 'Essex and the sugar slaves'; and 'Essex and slave emancipation'. There are several references to St. Kitts and on p. 55 Lewis tells of the Essex owner of slave-worked plantations in the West Indies – a family group descending from the Hon. William Mathew, who in 1752 devised to his grandson William Mathew of Great Baddow his plantations in St. Kitts. Reference is also made to the French landing on St. Kitts in 1782 and the manner in which Admiral Hood defeated du Grasse, restoring St. Kitts to Britain by treaty.

118 **Plantation life on Nevis.**
Jonathan Runge. In: *Rum and reggae: an alternative guide to the Caribbean.* London: Harrap-Columbus, 1990, p. 25-33. map.

Describes plantations of a past era when sugar was king, and observes the contemporary use of the great houses, for example, Montpelier Plantation, Nisbet Plantation Inn, Golden Rock, Croney's Old Manor Estate, and Zetland Plantation.

119 **St. Kitts, 1713-1763: a study of the development of a plantation colony.**
Margaret Deanne Rouse-Jones. Ann Arbor, Michigan: University
Microfilms, 1982. 229p. bibliog.

According to Rouse-Jones, 'the colonists had little attachment to the society and little interest . . . in viable and sturdy institutions . . . the dominant goals of the St. Kitts colonists were to further sugar monoculture and acquire profits'. This work discusses: the situation before the Treaty of Utrecht, 1624-1713; the failure of a planned society; economic and demographic growth; free and slave populations; the political system;

the established church in society; and social investment and development. The work concludes with an essay on sugar and society from 1713-63.

120   **Searching for the invisible woman.**
      Bridget Brereton.   *Slavery and Abolition*, vol. 13 (August 1992),
          p. 86-96.
Brereton reviews three publications by H. McD. Beckles, B. Bush and M. Morissey on the experience of Caribbean plantation slave women.

121   **The world an absentee planter and his slaves made: Sir William
      Stapleton and his Nevis sugar estate 1722-1740.**
      K. Mason.   *John Rylands University Library of Manchester Bulletin*,
          vol. 75, no. 1 (Spring 1993), p. 103-31. bibliog.
Mason presents a case-study of absenteeism, involving the Stapleton family, the overseer and Balls Range estate on Nevis in the 1720s. The study reveals the lack of communication between Stapleton and his managers, and its consequences.

The geological history of Mt. Misery volcano, St. Kitts, West Indies.
See item no. 27.

The Christena disaster in retrospect: error, challenge and hope.
See item no. 33.

West India sketch book.
See item no. 52.

Pocket guide to the West Indies.
See item no. 62.

Precis of information concerning the Presidency of Saint Christopher.
See item no. 109.

Caribbean Quakers.
See item no. 147.

Handbook of churches in the Caribbean.
See item no. 152.

Strings and pipe.
See item no. 157.

West Indian societies.
See item no. 163.

The potters of Nevis.
See item no. 449.

Crossing the river.
See item no. 459.

Guns of Dragonard.
See item no. 461.

Population and Ethnic Groups

122 **Caribbean ethnicity revisited.**
Edited by Stephen Glazier. New York, London, Paris, Tokyo: Gorgon & Breach Science Publishers, 1985. 164p.

This timely selection of papers, by a number of eminent anthropologists, explores the patterns of ethnicity in the Caribbean and provides a fascinating and vital study of the region as a whole. It focuses on the structure and behaviour of major ethnic groups: French and Puerto Ricans, immigrant whites and blacks from the US mainland and West Indians, including Kittitians and Nevisians, from the surrounding Eastern Caribbean.

123 **Demographic Yearbook.**
Department of Economic and Social Affairs, Statistical Office. New York: United Nations, 1948- . annual.

This yearbook carries statistics on population for almost every country in the world. Categories of figures include birth and death rates, migration, marriages and related issues, and the composition of households.

124 **Population census of the Commonwealth Caribbean, 1980-1981 (multi-volume).**
Caribbean Community and Common Market (CARICOM), Economic Commission for Latin American and Caribbean Countries (ECLAC). Port of Spain, Trinidad: CARICOM/ECLAC, 1985.

Volume three of this multi-volume work deals with St. Kitts-Nevis. There are many statistical tables which hold demographic details of the country. The population of the islands is tabulated according to sex, age group and district and in another instance the population is shown by major division, single years of age and sex. Statistics are also given for: immigration; education; vocational training; race and religion; marital and union status and fertility; and housing services and the household arrangements of the country. The work is the coordinated effort of the Caribbean Community and

Common Market (CARICOM) and the Economic Commission for Latin American and Caribbean Countries (ECLAC) and the national office in St. Kitts-Nevis.

125 **Studies on population, development and the environment in the Eastern Caribbean; project report to the government of St. Kitts-Nevis.**
Bridgetown, Barbados: University of the West Indies, 1982. 208p.
Four Eastern Caribbean countries are included in this project, which was sponsored by the Institute for Social and Economic Research and UNESCO in 1979-81. The main objective is to provide guidelines for the management of limited resources in Barbados, St. Kitts-Nevis, St. Lucia, and St. Vincent, which are all small, heavily-populated countries. Emphasis is laid on environmental issues, the management of natural resources issues and perception studies.

Overseas Populations

126 **The British state and immigration 1945-5.**

Kenneth Lum. *Immigrants and Minorities*, vol. 8 (November 1989), p. 16, 74. bibliog.

The author throws new light on the 'Empire Windrush'. He discusses the escalating migration of West Indians (including Kittitians) to Britain and shows how race has become politicized.

127 **Caribbean immigration to the United States.**

Roy S. Bryce-Laporte, Delores M. Mortimer. Washington, DC: Research Institute on Immigration and Ethnic Studies, 1983. 208p. bibliog.

The work of fourteen contributors, all but one of Caribbean origin, is edited here by Bryce-Laporte and Mortimer, and constitutes one of the first publications of the Research Institute on Immigration and Ethnic Studies since its establishment in 1973. It covers a wide range of related disciplines, including sociology, political science, anthropology, occupational therapy and international affairs. Each author brings a depth of experience and knowledge to the volume. An extensive bibliography provides further guidance on related issues, for example, race, ethnicity, assimilation and regional concerns. It is a useful source for the study of Caribbean immigration and related disciplines. A detailed and analytical review of the work appears in *The Review of Black Political Economy* (vol. 10, part 2, p. 223-35), by Simon B. Jones-Hendrickson who is a Kittitian and a professor at the Caribbean Research Institute, University of the Virgin Islands.

128 **Coloured minorities in Britain.**

Sydney Collins. London: Butterworth Press, 1957. 258p.

A collection of studies in British race relations based on African, Asiatic and West Indian immigrants. Kittitians and Nevisians are included in the study.

129 The coloured worker in the British industry.
Peter L. Wright. London: Oxford University Press, 1968. 245p.

Wright explains the backgrounds of coloured workers in Britain, their attitudes and aptitudes, their suitability and adaptability, their placements and discrimination against them, with special reference to immigrants in the Midlands and the north of England. There is a reasonable percentage of Kittitian immigrants in Britain.

130 Eastern Caribbean migrants in the United States of America: a demographic profile.
Averille White. *Bulletin of Eastern Caribbean Affairs*, vol. 13, no. 4 (September-October 1976). p. 8-28.

The demographic characteristics of the Eastern Caribbean migrants to the United States of America are described in this article. Information includes: country of birth; year of migration; age; educational attainment; and employment status. The data also indicates that although most migrants of Eastern Caribbean origin are employed, only a small proportion of persons hold professional occupations. Another relevant study of this subject is Simon Jones-Hendrickson's article, 'An empirical note on the spatial diffusion of nurses from the Commonwealth Caribbean to Britain' edited by Couch, Simon and Bryce-Laporte. (Research Institute on Immigration and Ethnic Studies, Research notes 2. Washington, DC: Smithsonian Institution, 1979, p. 221-37).

131 Far from home: the origin and significance of the Afro-Caribbean community in South Africa to 1950.
Alan Grego Cobley. *Journal of Southern African Studies*, vol. 18 (June 1992), p. 347-90. bibliog.

Cobley traces the origins of the Afro-Caribbean community (primarily seafarers) in South Africa. He analyses the character of this community and discusses its impact on black political consciousness and organization. There are tables which may indicate Kittitian-Nevisian references.

132 West Indians in Canada: the household-help scheme.
E. M. K. Douglas. *Social and Economic Studies*, vol. 17, no. 2 (June 1968), p. 215-17.

The author comments on the scheme outlined in the title, noting its pros and cons, the treatment of immigrants and how it affects their well-being in the country. It would be useful to compare this article with current findings.

133 West Indian migrants.
R. B. Davidson. London: Oxford University Press, 1962. 87p.

Davidson outlines and discusses the socio-economical factors of migration from the British West Indies. The work was carried out under the auspices of the Institute of Race Relations.

Migration

134   A bibliography of Caribbean migration and Caribbean immigrant communities.

Rosemary Brana-Shute.   Gainesville, Florida: University of Florida, 1983. 339p.

Arranged in standard form, this work lists acronyms and abbreviations, journal abbreviations, bibliographical entries and appendixes. Appendixes include: data bases searched; journals cited; the origins of migrants; the destinations of migrants; and a topical index. It should serve as a resourceful tool for: training new scholars; reviewing the existing state of knowledge in the subject; generating and disseminating research in priority areas; and for establishing collaborative relationships with other scholars and institutions. It should also be useful as an integrating mechanism and informational clearing house for research and forums.

135   Caribbean migrants: environment and human survival on St. Kitts-Nevis.

Bonham Richardson.   Knoxville, Tennessee: University of Tennessee Press, 1983. 209p.

An historical geography of human migration on St. Kitts-Nevis. It shows how Afro-Caribbean slaves and their descendants have creatively dealt with environmental and human-induced problems. It also discusses how generations of migrants from St. Kitts-Nevis have created an historical continuum and migration ethos which underlines today's societies.

136   Children's attitudes to the island community: the after-math of out-migration on Nevis.

Karen F. Olwig.   In: *Land and development.*   Edited by Jean Besson, Janet Momsen.   London: Macmillan, 1987, p. 153-69.

Questions the broad applicability of the assumption that an important basis for the existence of a nation is a certain innate attachment to the native land. It also questions the developmental strategy towards nationhood in some Caribbean islands. Problems associated with creating an independent, local, social and economic system on Nevis, where mass-emigration has resulted in a dependent, fragmented society, are discussed. The role of children's attitudes to Nevis prior to independence is also highlighted.

137 **Determinants and consequences of the migration culture of St. Kitts-Nevis.**
Frank L. Mills.   St.Thomas, Virgin Islands: University of the Virgin Islands, 1985. 83p.
Areas covered by this study are: methodological issues; the characteristics of migration from St. Kitts-Nevis; how and why emigration takes place; government policy on emigration; and recommendations.

138 **Emigration, remittances and social change: aspects of the social field of Nevis, West Indies.**
Richard Frucht.   *American Anthropologica*, vol. 10, pt. 2 (1968), p. 193-208.
Frucht defines the social field concept as 'the realisation of the importance of extra-local variables in understanding culture change and stability in primitive and peasant communities'. Following a brief description and history of Nevis, he looks at: the pattern of migration and social class; migration and social change; emigration; remittances; and the changing social field. There are useful references at the end of the article.

139 **Migration from Nevis since 1950.**
Carolyn Liburd.   Kingston, Jamaica: University of the West Indies, 1984. 73p.
This is an examination of migration from Nevis since 1950 and its effects on the Nevisian society. Prefaced by an historical background to Caribbean migration prior to 1950, the study covers patterns of migration, the characteristics of migrants and the contribution that could be made by migrants on return to their homeland. The migratory process is evaluated.

140 **Situations in St. Kitts-Nevis that promote migration: a predictive model.**
Frank L. Mills.   St. Thomas, Virgin Islands: University of the Virgin Islands, 1987. 29p.
According to the model used, the location and employment status are significant factors in the identification of potential migrant households. The chances of migration in households with a combination of response function characteristics are predicted. This paper was delivered at the International Congress of Caribbean Studies Association.

Historical geography of St. Kitts-Nevis: the West Indies.
See item no. 19.

Migration

Eastern Caribbean migrants in the United States of America: a demographic profile.
See item no. 130.

Culture, race and class in the Commonwealth Caribbean.
See item no. 160.

Social structure of the British Caribbean.
See item no. 162.

Annual digest of statistics for 1982.
See item no. 254.

Language and Dialects

141 A bibliography on the Creole language of the Caribbean, including a special supplement on Gullah.
Compiled by Roberto Nodal.   Milwaukee, Wisconsin: University of Wisconsin, Department of Afro-American Studies, 1972. 53p.

In this bibliography, there are entries on the whole of the Caribbean region. Many of the citations are annotated and include periodical articles.

142 Caribbean and African languages: social history, language and literature and education.
Morgan Dalphines.   London: Karia Press, 1985. 288p. bibliog.

Topics such as the social history of Creole languages, oral literature, the teaching of English as a second language and Creole in adult education are discussed with conviction and enthusiasm. Recommendations for the productive use of Creole in teaching are also given.

143 West Indians and their language.
Peter A. Roberts.   Cambridge, England: Cambridge University Press; University of the West Indies, Unit of use of English and linguistics, 1988. 215p. bibliog.

Following a general introduction, this study treats areas such as: language and varieties in the West Indies; Creole English; the linguistic sources of West Indian English; language and culture; and language in formal education. The work caters for the non-specialist but the educated reader who is seeking a comprehensive but succinct study of West Indian speech will also find it useful. References to St. Kitts-Nevis are on p. 3, 8, 9, 85, 87, 89, 95, 100-01, 103, 148 and 150.

Folklore

144 The folklore of St. Christopher's island.
Lloyd Matheson.   Basseterre, St. Kitts: Creole Graphics, 1985. 15p.
This booklet gives an account of the folklore of Kittitians. Reference is made to: maypole dancing; All Souls' day; Guy Fawkes' night; Shombololo bands; big drums; actors; mummies; the bull play; moko-jumbies; cakewalks, etc. The data provided will be useful to creative and folklore groups, dance groups, drama groups, calypsonians and short story writers, and will enable them to recreate the past and chart the future in ways peculiar to their distinctive disciplines.

145 Saint George and John Canoe.
Samuel M. Wilson.   *Natural History*, vol. 100 (December 1991), p. 22-27.
Christmas traditions in the Caribbean differ from island to island, and pageants combine legends from varied ancestral influences. The origins of several of the islands' masquerade characters are explored in this article, for example, John Canoe of Jamaica and Saint George of Nevis.

The independent way for St. Kitts.
See item no. 9.

Christmases past in Nevis.
See item no. 439.

The living arts and crafts of the West Indies.
See item no. 446.

Anansesem.
See item no. 451.

Our national heritage in prose and verse.
See item no. 473.

Religion

146 Black churches: West Indian and African sects in Britain.
Cliffton Hill.   London: Community and Race Relations Institute of
Britain, 1971. 23p.

Hill describes the churches in their locations and notes their contribution to the social
and cultural well-being of their congregations and communities. An earlier work,
'West Indian migrants and the London churches', 1963, also evokes the struggles of
settling and coping with the ordeal of living in a strange land.

147 Caribbean Quakers.
Harriet Frorer Durham.   Hollywood, Florida: Dukane Press, 1972.
133p. maps. bibliog.

An overview of the history of the Quakers in the West Indies. It begins in 1650 and
traces the Quakers' arrival, successes and trials up to the present day. References to
St. Kitts are on p. 37, 98, and 114; those to Nevis can be found on p. 16, 34, 39-40,
98, and 114.

**148 The Christian Council and Evangelical Association call for fresh
elections.**
Basseterre, St. Kitts: St. Kitts Christian Council, 1994. 1p.

This short publication documents the statements and convictions of the Christian
church in the aftermath of the St. Kitts-Nevis general election in December 1993. It
calls 'all leaders, supporters of political parties and the public in general to put the
interest of the Nation above Party and personal considerations, bearing in mind the
motto of the Federation – "Country above self"'.

149 **The church in the West Indies.**
A. Caldecott. London: Society for the Promotion of Christian
Knowledge, 1898. 275p. map.

An informative history of the Church of England in the West Indies. It describes the
work of the Anglicans as well as that of other churches, and relates the churches'
progress to other aspects of colonial development in the islands.

150 **A divine condition or a human tradition?**
DeVere Murrell. *Caribbean Contact*, vol. 19, no. 1 (December 1992
– January 1993), p. 12-13.

According to Murrell, the thirty-first Provincial Synod of the Anglican Church, which
took place in Barbados on 8-12 November 1992, dealt with a wide range of issues
including the controversial issue of the ordination of women. The Synod was unable
to find the two-thirds majority required to move forward as a province. One side of
the discussion argues 'that women's ordination is not a matter of equality of the
sexes, but rather a misunderstanding of their roles; that the male priesthood is rooted
in the theology and history of the church'. The opposite side argues that 'the maleness
of Christ and reference to God in masculine terms cannot be seen as a reason to
exclude women from the priesthood . . . Deity is conceptualised in terms of one's
environment . . . Jesus made revolutionary contact with women in a patriarchal
society and when the crisis came it was the women who gathered under the cross
while the men ran away . . . women can play a role in the church at its highest level'.

151 **Ecumenism and development: a socio-historical analysis of the
Caribbean Conference of Churches.**
Robert W. M. Cuthbert. Bridgetown, Barbados: Caribbean
Conference of Churches, 1986. 137p. map. bibliog.

An outstanding work, which seeks to document the experience of bringing together
Caribbean Churches within a single organization, and which focuses on the work of
the organization. The chapters, which treat the subject in great depth, have the
following headings: the Caribbean: a socio-anthropological profile; the rise of
organizational and leadership patterns in Caribbean Churches; Caribbean
organizational precursors and goal-setting for the Caribbean Conference of Churches;
the emergence of the CCC as a Caribbean Institution; the development fund: an
evaluation; and Conclusion. Appendixes include: Caribbean Conference of Churches
By-Laws (revised); a message from the fourth assembly of the World Conference of
Churches; and approximately fifteen tables.

152 **Handbook of churches in the Caribbean.**
Lisa Bessil-Watson. Georgetown, Barbados: The Cedar Press,
Caribbean Conference of Churches, 1982. 132p.

This popular and useful publication details the history of twelve churches, and gives
statistical data, and the names and addresses of theological colleges in the region.

153 **Need to perfect Caribbean ecumenism.**
Adolfo Ham. *Caribbean Contact*, vol. 18, no. 13 (July-August 1993), p. 4, 15.

Ham develops and argues the case for the need to perfect Caribbean ecumenism, by focusing on the mandate of the Caribbean Conference of Churches (CCC). He also pays attention to the vision of Methodist lay person Dr. John R. Mott (1865-1955), founder of the World's Student Christian Federation, the International Missionary Council, of many regional councils, and the World Council of Churches, and to the work of Robert Bilheimer and others. He draws on the wisdom of the New Testament and on the founders of the CCC 'to serve in the cause of unity, renewal and joint action, and to stimulate programmes of study, research and experimentation'. He asks whether the churches in the Caribbean are 'a growing body', renewing itself constantly, and whether they are fostering or dismantling Afro-Caribbean culture, and calls for the launch of a study project on the relationship between the churches and culture.

154 **Real roots and potted plants: reflections on the Caribbean Church.**
Ashley Smith.   Williamsfield, Jamaica: Mandeville Publishers, 1984. 91p.

This collection of papers delivered over a thirteen-year span analyses the effectiveness of the Church's ministry to the Caribbean people. The author emphasizes the need for people to break free of the forces of spiritual enslavement, and he addresses the Church's task in social change and renewal, justice and development, liberation, faith and economics, changing systems and hope. This book is a critical look at the Church in the emergent Caribbean by a qualified and experienced insider who lectures at the Theological College of the West Indies, Jamaica. This book is applicable to the entire Caribbean region, including St. Kitts-Nevis.

155 **The role of the Sephardic Jews in the British Caribbean during the 17th century.**
G. Merrill. *Caribbean Studies*, vol. 4, no. 3 (October 1964), p. 32-49.

In the section of this article entitled 'Sephardic Jewish cultures in St. Kitts-Nevis', Merrill traces their work and influence in the islands.

156 **Souvenir booklet giving thanks to God for the Conference of the Methodist Church in the Caribbean and the Americas celebrating its 21st Meeting.**
Belmont, Antigua: Methodist Church in the Caribbean and the Americas, 1987. 51p.

Twenty years of Methodism in the Caribbean, run by the region's own Conference, instead of the centuries' old London Methodist Missionary Society, is a considerable achievement. The reflections of forty-two Caribbean men of God on the development of a significant Conference make informative and soul-stirring reading. One of John Wesley's quotations: 'the best of all is God is with us', the Conference and Church's crests, and photographs of the headquarters of the Conference in Antigua embellish the cover.

157   **Strings and pipe.**
    G. P. J. Walker.   [n.p.], 1987. 6p.
The story of the building of an organ on the island of St. Kitts in the year 1872.

Now hear the word of the Lord.
See item no. 12.

Ecocentrism not anthropocentrism.
See item no. 359.

Caribbean Journal of Religious Studies.
See item no. 522.

Social Structure

158 **Afro-Caribbean men: an endangered species?**
    C. M. Hope. *Caribbean Contact*, vol. 19, no. 9 (September 1993),
    p. 1, 6-11, 14-17, 19.
Several writers have contributed to the overall theme in this issue. The editorial (p. 1)
'Marginalisation of young black men' by C. M. Hope, claims that 'there is a glass
ceiling over the aspirations of all black men . . . when societies consciously confront
this bleak fact . . . they will build their own structures which will challenge and
compete against the prevailing unjust world in which the whole black race is
imprisoned'. Other contributions are: p. 6-9, 'Marginalisation – the crisis facing Afro-
Caribbean male youth' by Maureen Benjamin; p. 10-11, 'The real problem of Afro-
Caribbean male youth: a feminist perspective', by Gemma Tang Nain; and p. 14-19,
'What is happening to our young men?' by Kael Tafari.

159 **Crab antics: social anthropology of English speaking Negro**
    societies of the Caribbean.
    Peter J. Wilson.   New Haven, Connecticut: Yale University Press,
    1973. 258p. (Caribbean Series, 14).
Wilson sets out to provide an analysis of the 'moral life' of Caribbean society. He
identifies and analyses the criteria and standards by which people judge each other's
worth and explains how values of social differentiation provide a basis for social
order. Reference is made to St. Kitts on p. 192, concerning an incident with Governor
Woodley and the inhabitants in 1770. The author concludes that 'fundamental matters
of social and moral values' should be given equal consideration with economics, in
respect of societal problems. There is an appendix showing the relationship between
food and social status.

160 **Culture, race and class in the Commonwealth Caribbean.**
    M. G. Smith, foreword by Rex Nettleford. Mona, Jamaica:
    University of the West Indies, Department of Extra Mural Studies,
    1984. 163p.

Smith reviews various accounts of Anglo-Caribbean societies from 1945 to the present, and discusses the part that culture, race and class play in them. The work seeks to assess the collective contribution of these studies and to clarify the critical issues and realities with which they deal. Although attention focuses on four particular West Indian societies, the book also presents general models which could be applied to St. Kitts-Nevis, for they are also of that 'distinctive socio-eco order determined by experiences and historical formation rooted in the chattel slavery and plantation system'.

161 **The growth of the modern West Indies.**
    Gordon K. Lewis. New York: Monthly Review Press, 1968. 506p.

A brilliant analysis and interpretation of modern West Indian society. It is comprehensive in scope and scholarly in treatment, analysing in detail the character of the various elements that make up the whole of West Indian society.

162 **Social structure of the British Caribbean.**
    George Cumber. Millwood, New York: Kraus Reprint Company,
    1978. 90p.

A thorough treatment of the subject, which deals with topics such as population and vital statistics of the British West Indies in general, individual islands in particular, inter-colonial immigration, housing and racial groups. There is much tabulated information with historical comparisons, for example, the population table on p. 9 includes census figures for St. Kitts-Nevis. Table 2 shows the gainfully employed population by industry groups and colonies and another table indicates colonial immigration by age and sex. Originally published by the Extra Mural Department of the University of the West Indies, this is recommended reading for anyone who wishes to gain an insight into the general background of the social structure of the islands.

163 **West Indian societies.**
    D. Lowenthal. London: Oxford University Press, 1972. 385p.
    bibliog.

An overview of social structure in the West Indies, stressing the historic and current situations in each territory. There are several references to Nevis and St. Kitts.

The social impact of tourism in Nevis.
See item no. 67.

Free coloureds in the slave societies of St. Kitts and Grenada, 1763-1833.
See item no. 114.

Emigration, remittances and social change: aspects of the social field of Nevis, West Indies.
See item no. 138.

Migration from Nevis since 1950.
See item no. 139.

Ecumenism and development: a socio-historical analysis of the Caribbean Conference of Churches.
See item no. 151.

Social Conditions

164 **Community and context in a colonial society: social and economic change in Nevis.**
Richard Frucht.   Ann Arbor, Michigan: University Microfilms, 1982. 205p.

Frucht's work is arranged into three main sections. Part one consists of: the introduction; chapter one – problem and methodology; and chapter two – the geography and population of contemporary Nevis, physical geography, cultural geography, and island population. Part two, 'Historical changes in Nevis economy and society' contains chapters three to five, which deal respectively with: economic decline, the introduction of cotton production, and political changes; changes in the organization of production; and changes in land tenure. Part three, 'Social and economical change in contemporary Nevis', is dealt with in chapter six – the marketing of sea-island cotton. Each section ends with a précis of its chapters.

165 **Eastern Caribbean Drug Service Policy Board: a report.**
Castries, St. Lucia: Organisation of Eastern Caribbean States (OECS), 1989. 12p.

Eight papers were presented at the meeting held in Montserrat on 27-28 April 1989. They discussed, among other subjects: the obtainability of medical supplies; pharmaceuticals; health services; and health facilities.

166 **Living conditions: a social issue in St. Kitts.**
Mavis V. Webster.   Basseterre, St. Kitts: St. Kitts Teachers Training College, [n.d.]. vii, 32p.

The Kittitian housing situation is presented as a grave social concern. Webster provides some suggestions for correcting the situation.

167 **Making sense of the Caribbean drug traffic: how the cocaine merchants opportunistically piggy-back on the traditional ganja routes.**
Canute James. *West Indian Digest*, no. 159 (November 1988), p. 12-13.
James describes the ways in which drugs are being shipped, for example, by illegal airstrips, boats and air-craft island hopping. He also tells of some raids and describes how more emphasis is now being placed on fighting drug abuse, particularly in high schools, and on increased police surveillance.

168 **Marijuana: the drug problem in St. Kitts.**
Jesica O. Nisbett. Basseterre, St. Kitts: St. Kitts Teachers Training College, [n.d.]. 25p.
Gives an insight into the existing marijuana problems in St. Kitts and on the international level. Recommendations to assist in the national solution of the problem are suggested.

169 **Poverty and progress in the Caribbean, 1800-1960.**
J. R. Ward. London; Basingstoke, England: Macmillan, 1985. 82p. bibliog.
This should serve as a springboard to future work; it provides access to the best work carried out in this area and helps users draw their own conclusions in major fields of study. One of the topics in which St. Kitts-Nevis is featured appears on p. 31-34 under the heading 'Adjustments to Emancipation'.

170 **Problems of alcoholism in St. Kitts.**
Randolph A. Gardener. Basseterre, St. Kitts: St. Kitts Teachers Training College, [n.d.]. 24p.
Discusses the dangers of alcoholism and its effects on society, and offers recommendations to help afflicted individuals.

171 **St. Kitts-Nevis Director of Social Security elected to the ISSA Bureau.**
Labour Spokesman, vol. 35, no. 64 (30 December 1992), p. 5.
According to this article regarding the twenty-fourth General Assembly of the International Social Security Association (ISSA), the titular delegate of St. Kitts-Nevis Social Security Board was elected to ISSA's Board of Directors. This is the first time since ISSA was founded in 1927 that a person of the English-speaking Caribbean has been elected to the Bureau. Over 1,000 delegates from 111 countries attended the General Assembly. The aim of ISSA is to protect, promote and develop social security throughout the world.

172 **Some social and rural elements in contemporary Caribbean society.**

Whitman T. Browne.   Basseterre, St. Kitts: [n.p.], 198?, 9p.

Browne discusses certain elements in Caribbean societies which indicate that although some Caribbean countries boast nationalism and independence, their colonial past still influences their social processes. Eight such elements are: ambiguity and frustration over the role of labour unions; high levels of unemployment; a general tendency towards longevity; the misuse of the media; psychological dependency; conflict trends in emigration and immigration; political illiteracy; and increased evidence of emotional abnormality in society. Some rural elements are also examined: physical renewal; urban-rural migration; dynamic population growth; and marriage.

173 **Statement of youth challenges and problems in St. Kitts.**

A. E. Bridgewater.   Basseterre, St. Kitts: [n.p.], 1982. 4p.

Challenges facing the youth (aged 16-25) of St. Kitts are outlined and problems discussed. Some of the needs identified by the author are: to combat teenage pregnancy; to introduce a population development policy; to encourage the participation of young people in meaningful activities and programmes; to recognize youths' achievements; and to provide varied opportunities for them.

174 **Teenage pregnancy in the Caribbean.**

Tirbani Jagdeo.   New York: Inter-American Parliamentary Group on Population and Development, 1985. 12p.

This work deals with the situation of family planning in the Caribbean generally and presents a plea for action.

175 **Welfare and planning in the West Indies.**

T. S. Simey.   Oxford: Clarendon Press, 1946. 267p. map.

The origins, organization, economic foundations and rebuilding of West Indian society are the engaging topics which are discussed in this work. It includes results of inquiries into vital statistics, the cost of living, land use and economic-organization situations.

Essay on St. Kitts.
See item no. 7.

Medicine and Health

General and regional

176 **Afro Caribbean folk medicine: the reproduction and practice of healing.**
Michel S. Laguerre.   Granby, Massachusetts: Garvey Publishers Inc., 1987. 120p. bibliog.

This important study analyses and introduces some conceptual order into the vast domain of Caribbean folk beliefs and practices. Among the topics it covers are: the evolution of slave medicine; the transmission of folk medicine knowledge; the practitioners; body, blood and illness; and faith healing. There are four useful appendices: a sample of African plants brought to the Caribbean by slave ships; medicinal plants used by Caribbean slaves; food items with hot and cold qualities; and a sample of medicinal plants used in the Caribbean. Fifteen Caribbean islands are analysed and the author attempts to provide a better understanding of a persisting folk medicine tradition not generally known. He is the associate Professor of Caribbean Studies at the University of California.

177 **Aids: a broadcast.**
Earl S. Morris.   Basseterre, St Kitts-Nevis. Ministry of Health, 1987. 10p.

Morris alerts citizens and residents of St. Kitts-Nevis of the dangers of AIDS and how not to contract it. He defines the disease and offers twelve guidelines to limit the risk of infection.

178 **Alcohol in a Caribbean perspective: a case study of the roles of beverage alcohol in Nevis, West Indies.**
Lenore Ralston.   San Francisco, California: Medical Research of San Francisco, 1982. 215p.

Focuses on the inter-relationships between the tourist industry, the alcohol beverage industry and the local rates of alcohol-related problems. The study covers areas such as: alcohol availability in St. Kitts; alcohol and the law; public health and alcohol-related problems; tourism; economics; and their impact on the local population. The views and observations of a cross-section of Nevisians on the role of alcohol in the community are recorded.

179 **Annual medical and sanitary report for the year 1927.**
St. Kitts, Nevis and Anguilla Medical Officer.   Basseterre, St. Kitts: St. Kitts, Nevis and Anguilla Medical Department, 1928. 70p.

Reviews the general medical state of the country in 1927, and is useful for retrospective study. It presents details on: vital statistics; general diseases; communicable diseases; nutrition; housing; sanitation; maternal and child health; dental care; quarantine; and finance. It records the total number of operations performed at the Alexandra Hospital, Nevis, for the year as being 141.

180 **Annual medical and sanitary report for the year 1952.**
St. Kitts, Nevis and Anguilla Medical Officer.   Basseterre, St. Kitts: St. Kitts, Nevis and Anguilla Medical Department, 1953. 137p.

A report of historical value, that records notable progress in medical work in both the curative and preventative fields. The death rate (12.8 per 1,000 population) was the lowest ever recorded in the country (records date back to 1859). In addition to the usual sections, the report highlights: health centres and outposts; district medical services; hospitals; leper homes; the care of the aged and infirm; port health and quarantine; laboratory service; legislation; and finance. Appendixes include: vital statistics; summary statistics for the past five years; detailed statistics for 1952; the classification of hospital in-patients, 1952; the classification of new cases seen by medical officers; the work of V.D. and Yaws clinics; and tuberculosis deaths, 1943-52. Reports are published annually and are available from the St. Kitts-Nevis Medical Department, Basseterre, St. Kitts.

181 **Baby Saving League and Child Welfare, St. Kitts: a report.**
Basseterre, St. Kitts: Baby Saving League and Child Welfare, 1925. 17p.

This historic document records the work of the St. Kitts Baby Saving League and Child Welfare Society, which is affiliated with the West Indian Health and Welfare Society, London, 1922. It covers the period from 1st October 1923 to 30th September 1924, and includes financial statements. The Baby Saving League and Child Welfare Society was founded by Mrs J. A. Burdon in 1921.

182   **Caribbean contraceptive prevalence surveys.**
      Tirbani Jagdeo.   New York: International Planned Parenthood
      Federation, 1985. 102p.

Determines and clarifies the levels of contraceptive use in St. Kitts-Nevis. The survey
also assesses the effectiveness of information, education and delivery services on
patterns of contraceptive use in the country.

183   **Caribbean Council for the Blind.**
      Kevin Carey.   St. John's, Antigua: Caribbean Council for the Blind,
      1980. 53p.

Carey has assembled here a workable programme for sight conservation and work
with blind persons in the CARICOM region for the period 1980-89. Sub-branches of
the Council, sometimes called 'Friends of the Blind', exist throughout the islands.
Carey, the Director of the Council, travels throughout the Caribbean to introduce
appropriate programmes and to encourage participants.

184   **Commonwealth Caribbean Medical Resource Council proceedings
      of a scientific meeting.**
      West Indian Medical Research Council.   Kingston, Jamaica: The
      author, 1989. 84p.

This supplement to the *West Indian Medical Journal* records the deliberations of a
meeting held on 19-22 April 1989. It includes a list of on-going research topics and
reports on new medical trends in the region.

185   **Control of diabetes mellitus in the Caribbean Community.**
      Caribbean Food and Nutrition Institute.   Kingston, Jamaica:
      Caribbean Food and Nutrition Institute, 1986. 115p.

The formula for the control of diabetes mellitus was established at a workshop on the
standardization of the management of diabetes mellitus and hypertension in the entire
Caribbean community, held in St. Lucia from 26-28 May 1986. Several illustrations,
tables, diagrams and charts help to clarify the work and to enable comparisons
between the islands.

186   **Effect of family life education on knowledge, onset of sexual
      activity and contraceptive use.**
      Tulane University.   Basseterre, St. Kitts: Ministry of Education,
      Health and Community Affairs, [n.d.]. 6p.

A research project to assess the influence of family life education was tested on six
government high schools in St. Kitts-Nevis. The sex education component seeks to
discover the sexual activity of teenagers of high school age, their knowledge and use
of contraceptives and the incidence of pregnancy among them. The findings show that
the students' knowledge of reproductive anatomy, physiology and contraceptives had
improved but that the programme affected neither their sexual activity nor the use of
contraceptives among sexually active teenagers.

187 **Evaluation in developing countries: a case study of the St. Kitts teenage family life education programme.**
Rita Goldfarb O'Sullivan.   Auburn University, 1984.
It is assumed that for developing countries, the evaluation approach is more responsive than a prescribed methodology. This study tests that assumption.

188 **Health in the Eastern Caribbean.**
Cora Christian.   Charlotte Amalie, St. Thomas, US Virgin Islands: Caribbean Studies Association, 1981.
The health care delivery of St. Kitts-Nevis is one of three of the OECS countries which the author assesses and compares with the health care delivery of the United States Virgin Islands. The systems are assessed in terms of their socio-economic, geographical, political, and technical resources and the structure of the countries' health care delivery. Indicators of health such as birth, death, and infant mortality rates were used and analysed according to government expenditure, bed capacity and number of medical staff. Christian concludes that the proportion of money spent on health over a period of time was the only factor that had a consistent relationship to improved health status.

189 **National nursing policies for St. Kitts-Nevis.**
Gloria Noel.   Basseterre, St. Kitts: Ministry of Education, Health and Community Affairs, [n.d.]. 113p.
Noel discusses how regional nursing standards are used to develop local policies, which are based on: national public service laws and regulations; general nursing council rules; and regulations. Recommendations include working conditions, nursing codes, administration, personnel, service and legislation.

190 **Psychological needs and cultural systems: a case study.**
Joel Aronoff.   Leiden, Netherlands; New York: Van Nostrand, 1967. 241p. bibliog. (Insight Books no. 36).
Analyses the social psychology in the context of historical and existing social conditions, and examines traditional cultural systems and how they affect the psyche. The work also points to the strengths and weaknesses of cultural systems, discovers some psychological needs and suggests some methods of improvement.

191 **Qualitative study of male attitudes in St. Kitts-Nevis.**
New York: International Planned Parenthood Federation, [n.d.].
The findings of this study, which looks at male contraceptive attitudes, show that male attitudes are dictated by societal norms and acceptance. When society condones multiple relationships, a family life where fathers may have 'outside' children is reinforced. Samples of age groups used are: 5-18; 18-25; and 25-35.

192 **The role of the community in primary health care.**
Alphonso A. Bridgewater.   Basseterre, St. Kitts: Primary Health Care Workshop, 1982. 9p.
Discusses the basic concepts and components of primary health care and outlines the community's responsibility. Bridgewater describes primary health care as an

alternative to the institutionally oriented physician-based health care. Findings reveal that the most important health factors are: drainage; the removal of refuse from habitations, streets and roads; and the improvement of the water supply. It recommends the following for improved primary health care: a comprehensive education strategy including activities to provide individuals with the knowledge, skills and attitudes which will enable them to lead a satisfactory life in the community.

Mental health

193 Attitudes towards disabled children in St. Kitts.

Brenda Davies. *Conquest Quarterly Magazine*, vol. 1, no. 3 (June-September 1989), p. 3-4.

Davies describes her findings under four headings: the attitudes of the family; the attitude of society; the attitude of the Government; and attitudes within the civil service. This magazine is sponsored by Disabled Peoples International North American and Caribbean Region.

194 Mental illness: a social issue in St. Kitts.

Verlyn Claxton-Maynard. Basseterre, St. Kitts: St. Kitts-Nevis Teachers Training College, [n.d.]. 12p.

Types of mental illnesses and their characteristics are discussed in this short work, and recommendations regarding the treatment of mentally ill persons in the community are offered.

195 Operation Childfind.

Brenda Davies. *Conquest Quarterly Magazine*, vol. 1, no. 3 (June-September 1989), p. 12.

This important survey locates 106 disabled children (six sight impaired, nineteen hearing impaired, and the rest physically or mentally handicapped or both) in St. Kitts-Nevis. Some problems are identified and suggestions made to the Association for Handicapped Children.

Saint Christopher and Nevis Constitution Order 1983.
See item no. 237.

St. Kitts Biomedical Research Foundation conducts studies.
See item no. 436.

Caribbean Family Planning Affiliation Report.
See item no. 518.

Caribbean Nurses Association.
See item no. 525.

Women's Affairs

196 **Caribbean women: their history and habits.**
G. K. Osei.   London: African Publication Society, 1979. 191p.
bibliog.

Through this chronicle of roles and moods which are rooted in the past and living history of the region, the author shows how the Caribbean woman has taken her place alongside the man in building a Caribbean society and nation. It is an 'epic [of the] suffering and glorious achievement of Caribbean women'.

197 **The International Women's Association of St. Kitts (IWAS) celebrates its tenth anniversary.**
Dorothy M. Pertha.   *The Labour Spokesman*, (23 February 1994), p. 6.

Pertha explains the function and activities of the International Women's Association of St. Kitts (IWAS) as the organization celebrates ten years of involvement with the community: 'It is a circle of ladies who stand ready to help new arrivals become part of the St. Kitts community'. IWAS works on projects like improving the quality of life for residents in the Cardin Home, the Children's Home, the Harris Home and the Home for Disabled Children. Almost every country is represented: women from China, the USA, Korea, Ghana, Costa Rica, Sri Lanka, Canada, the UK, Jakarta and Greece have all brought their own 'flavour' to St. Kitts and have produced a popular cookbook, now in its third edition.

198 **The role of women in the development of small economies – lesson from the Caribbean.**
Joycelin Massiah.   Basseterre, St. Kitts: Commonwealth Secretariat, Eastern Caribbean Central Bank, 1991.

In this study, Massiah makes four basic statements: that regardless of size, sovereign states are confronted with the basic task of improving the standard of living of all their people; that regardless of size, societies all over the world require women to perform a multiplicity of roles, intended to maintain social cohesion; that the ability of women to perform these roles effectively is integrally related to the sensitivity of the socio-economic environment in which they live; and that in development circles in the Caribbean community, the idea of people rather than state-led development has recently taken root. The author then attempts to assess current policies and institutional measures which affect women and to suggest measures for introducing a more gender-sensitive approach to economic planning and development in the Commonwealth Caribbean.

199 **Selected bibliography of materials and resources on women in the Caribbean available at WAND's research and documentation centre.**
Diane Innis. Bridgetown, Barbados: University of the West Indies, Women and Development (WAND), 1988. 97p.
An excellent tool for locating teaching aids, organizations and human resources available on women's affairs in the Caribbean.

200 **Working miracles, women of the English speaking Caribbean.**
Olive Senior. London: James Currey, 1992. 224p.
Using a wide range of source material, including literature and popular culture, Senior examines the lives and works of women in the Caribbean. It is a useful source book for anyone interested in women's studies and the Caribbean.

201 **Women-vigilant and visionary (The Caribbean woman).**
C. M. Hope. *Caribbean Contact*, vol. 19, no. 10 (October 1993), p. 2.
This editorial emphasizes that 'Caribbean women have taken the intellectual and organisational offensive in the search for redressing historical imbalances and identifying a progressive path for societies'. Hope lists the varieties of feminist theories as indicated in the extensive Caribbean literature available today, and detects a political commitment to changing women's position in their societies. In conclusion, the editor states that 'the struggle for equal rights and justice for women is a community effort that resides at the core of the terms "progress" and "development".' Other contributions to the theme in this issue are: 'In support of West Indies women cricketers', by Hilary Beckles; 'Women making strides', by Gail Alexander; 'Ismene Krisnadath – writing for development', by Bianca Mohamamatsaid-Zalman; 'Winning Williams', by David Cuffy; 'Convictions of a churchwoman', by June Johnston; 'Condition of women in the media has not improved', by Margaret Harris; 'Poor women playing vital role', by Suzanne Burke; 'Women separated by miles', by Maria Baah; and 'Violation of women's rights continues in the Caribbean', excerpts from a paper by Roberta Clarke at the Global Tribunal on Violations against Women (Vienna, June 1991). The entire issue constitutes a significant contribution to the re-evaluation of the place of the Caribbean woman.

Human Rights

202 **Geopolitics of the Caribbean: ministates in a wider world.**
Thomas Anderson. New York: Praeger; Stanford, California: Hoover
Institution Press, 1984. 174p. maps. bibliog.

Contemporary geopolitical issues, including human rights practices and foreign
policy options in a region of change, are discussed against the geographical setting
and historical background of the Caribbean. Table seven – a comparative survey of
freedoms – grades political rights, civil rights and combined ratings in Caribbean
countries. St. Kitts-Nevis receives a combined rating indicating 'full freedom'. The
work provides an overview of the environment and the political geography of the
region, with a strong focus on the small Eastern Caribbean countries, including
St. Kitts-Nevis. It covers the general geographical setting, political entities,
economical base and historical background. In addition, it deals with marine
boundaries and the options.

203 **Human rights report, 1993.**
Washington, DC: USA Department of State, 1994.

The human rights practices of several Caribbean countries and of the United Kingdom
are listed and described. Countries under review are: Antigua and Barbuda; the
Bahamas; Barbados; United Kingdom; St. Kitts and Nevis; St. Lucia; St. Vincent;
Suriname; Trinidad and Tobago; Jamaica; Grenada; Guyana; Haiti; Belize; Dominica;
and the Dominican Republic. The article on St. Kitts-Nevis appears as no. 51 in 4133
words. The Human Rights Convention is attached as Appendix C.

Politics

204 **Bureaucratic activism and politicised bureaucracies as emerging strategies for development: St. Kitts-Nevis, a case study.**
Keith Simmonds. Basseterre, St. Kitts: Caribbean Studies Association, 1984. 26p.

The arguments put forth in this paper are that: political neutrality as a concept and practice will be seriously challenged by a new approach to bureaucratic activity; and that the nature and composition of the post-independence bureaucracy, and the government's goals for social change, will most likely cause the value of the political neutrality to shift significantly towards the force of an action-orientated bureaucracy.

205 **Caribbean and world politics: cross currents and cleavages.**
Edited by Jorge Heine, Leslie Manigat. New York: Holmes & Meir, 1988. 385p. bibliog.

Divided into four major sections, this comprehensive effort is the work of several contributors: 'Geopolitics and international political economy' by Leslie Manigat, Carl Stone, Mirlande Manigat and Trevor Farrell; 'Caribbean foreign policies: cases and courses' by Vaughan Lewis, Paul Ashley and Jean Crusol; 'The role of some regional middle powers' by Kari Levitt, Fernando Cepeda and Mirlande Manigat; and 'The United States and the Caribbean' by Edward Gonzales, Robert Pastor and Anthony Manigat. Additionally, there is an epilogue by Leslie Manigat and a bibliographical guide by Jorge Heine. There are several references to St. Kitts-Nevis.

206 **Closer union.**
Kennedy Simmonds. Basseterre, St. Kitts: St. Kitts-Nevis Government, 1987. 5p.

An address by the Prime Minister of St. Kitts-Nevis at an OECS summit held in Tortola, British Virgin Islands, on 27 May 1987. The politician calls for the establishment of mechanisms for the attainment of objectives which should be carefully analysed and presented to the people for study and comment.

207 **Concerned Citizens Movement Manifesto for 1993.**
Concerned Citizens Movement. *The Labour Spokesman*, (28 May
1993), p. 12.

An extract from the manifesto which articulates the Movement's principal concerns,
and broad objectives. It also sets out the CCM's views on the future of Nevis.

208 **From commoner to king: Robert Bradshaw, crusader for dignity
and justice in the Caribbean.**
Whitman T. Browne. Lanham, Maryland: University Press of
America, 1992, 425p. map. bibliog.

This full-length work focuses 'on the role of Robert Bradshaw (in politics) as he
supervised, then dominated, the emergence of working class politics in St. Kitts,
Nevis and Anguilla through the Labour Union movement from 1944 until 1978'.
Bradshaw, leader of the Labour Party at the time, became the first Premier of St.
Kitts-Nevis in 1967. Chapter headings are as novel as the material they summarize:
Beginnings, ideological orientations, reflections; A time when wrong was right; The
power of experience; Pillars for challenge and change; Issues of race, class and
culture; A battle for minds; Standing against the flow; Labour unionism; the early
years; From labour union to politics and beyond; Wearing two hats; These testify;
From colony to independent nation; Monarch of all surveyed; Then there were two;
Nevis and St. Kitts: to be or not to be; New bottles – old wine; One divided by eight;
Sceptre and crown; Unfading pictures; Legacies of time; and Hold strain. The author,
a Nevisian, contends that 'Bradshaw made sterling contributions to the evolution of
contemporary Caribbean politics up to the 1980s . . . he was a sincere and honest
Caribbean man as well as a committed Pan Africanist'. The work is essential reading
for students of Caribbean politics.

209 **Independence message to the Nation.**
Denzil Douglas. *The Labour Spokesman*, vol. 36, no. 33
(18 September 1993), p. 1, 3.

Reproduces the text of a radio address aired by the St. Kitts-Nevis Labour Party and
Leader of the Opposition in the National Assembly in St. Kitts-Nevis on the occasion
of the tenth anniversary of the Federation of St. Kitts-Nevis. The message highlights
the Labour Party's commitment to independence and 're-emphasises its further
commitment to end political tribalism' in the country.

210 **Interviews with Lee L. Moore.**
Dawud Bryan. Frederiksted, St. Croix, US Virgin Islands: Eastern
Caribbean Institute, 1989.

In fourteen candid interviews, Bryan helps Moore, a former Premier of St. Kitts-
Nevis, to bare the political and economical soul of his country. The problems and
prospects of St. Kitts-Nevis are revealed as is the Labour Party's all-embracing
developmental policy for the islands.

211 In this democracy? A look at the political system of St. Kitts and Nevis.
Lemuel Pemberton. Basseterre, St. Kitts: St. Kitts Teachers Training College, 1986.

An examination of the political system of the country. It traces the political history, examines definitions of democracy and indicates the population's views on democracy in St. Kitts-Nevis.

212 Law, power and government in St. Kitts, Nevis and Anguilla: politics and ambition clash in a mini-state.
Stogumber Brown. Basseterre, St. Kitts: Labour Spokesman Printery, 1980. 146p.

This work reviews the political background before St. Kitts, Nevis and Anguilla became an Associated State with Great Britain in 1967. It also outlines the aftermath of an abortive attempt to overthrow the Bradshaw government in St. Kitts (10th June 1967). The operation of the law at those times is observed with an analysis of the role and operations of the Court. The threats of a Nevisian secession and the role of the People's Action Movement (PAM) are examined.

213 Manifesto 1989.
People's Action Movement. Basseterre, St. Kitts: The People's Action Movement, 1989. 34p.

Records the achievements of the People's Action Movement for two terms of office and its action plan for a further term. Economic diversification with broad based areas is emphasized with particular reference to the following areas: agricultural and industrial development; tourism; infrastructure and services; housing; health; education; human resource development; youth and women's affairs; community development; the public service; legal reform; and security.

214 Modern Caribbean politics.
Anthony Payne, Paul Sutton. Kingston, Jamaica: Ian Randle Publishing, 1993. 332p. bibliog.

A general history of politics in the Caribbean. Revolution, democracy and regional integration are dealt with in chapter six by Tony Thorndike who covers the situation in St. Kitts-Nevis. Another relevant article is: 'A transformation process in the Caribbean' from *Caribbean issues of emergence: socio-economic and political prospectives*, edited by Vincent McDonald (Washington, DC: University Press of America, 1980, p. 69-94).

215 The negro in the Caribbean.
Eric Williams. Washington, DC: The Associates in Negro Folk Education, 1942. 119p. bibliog.

This analysis sets the West Indies in its historical past and presents problems in a challenging and constructive way. Although now somewhat dated, this work is still relevant in that it deals with solutions which will lead to the constructive enlargement of western democracy. A paperback edition was published in 1976.

216 **The Nevis local council: a case of formalism in structural change.**
Urias Forbes. *Caribbean Studies*, vol. 11, no. 2 (1971), p. 21-32.

Forbes deals exclusively with Nevis in this article and 'is concerned with the responsiveness of a small highly centralised administration, rooted in an authoritative past, in accommodating itself to change which purports to foster a type of administration based on a concept of wider popular involvement and participation'. More specifically, the article discusses the social and political trends which, prior to 1967, influenced the desire for decentralization within the framework of a local council.

217 **Party politics in the West Indies.**
Edited by C. L. R. James, foreword by R. M. Walters.   Imprint Caribbean Ltd., 1984. 184p.

First published in 1962 merely 'as a public statement' by a distinguished Caribbean writer on the local political scene. James's famous line, 'the people know that all is not well, that there are realities which all the talk does not touch', is an example of what makes this author 'the creative political theorist', so highly acclaimed on the international scene.

218 **Political changes in St. Kitts and Nevis.**
Bonham C. Richardson. *Geographical Review*, vol. 67, no. 3 (1977), p. 357-59.

Discusses several reasons why the St. Kitts government desired independence from Britain. It also states the suspicions and fears of Nevisians against St. Kitts and the concept of independence, and indicates the 'very serious' sentiment about secession from St. Kitts.

219 **Promise in the Caribbean: democratic breezes on St. Kitts-Nevis.**
Forrest Colburn. *The New Leader*, (August 1984), p. 12-13.

Doubts are raised regarding the stability and survival of the West Indian parliamentary governments which are based on the Westminister model. The situation in St. Kitts-Nevis is reviewed, and the author suggests convincingly that democracy in the twin nation, while highly vulnerable, is nevertheless viable. He describes local and regional party politics before concluding that 'there appears to be a growing appreciation . . . that the alternative to slow progress under democratic institutions is less likely to be more rapid revolutionary change than the reimposition of exploitive authoritarian rule'. Colburn is Assistant Professor of political science at Florida International University.

220 **Saint Kitts-Nevis: an uneasy alliance.**
Arthur Magida. *Islands International Magazine*, (July/August 1985). p. 66-77.

The political alliance between St. Kitts and Nevis is discussed in this article, which also touches on the special appeal which the islands hold for visitors.

221 **Seize the time: towards the Organisation of Eastern Caribbean States (OECS) Political Union.**
William G. Demas.   St. Michael, Barbados: Caribbean Development Bank, 1987. 57p.

Based on an address on political unity in the Eastern Caribbean, the President of the Caribbean Development Bank states in this document the case for wider political union in the West Indies. He answers such questions as: why it is necessary to start with the OECS; and which form of political unity it should take.

222 **Strategies for progress in the post-independent Caribbean: a Bradshawish synthesis.**
Simon Jones-Hendrickson.   St. Thomas, United States Virgin Islands: Caribbean Studies Association, 1984. 35p.

The 'Bradshawish synthesis' is discussed under the following headings: Bradshaw as an architect of Caribbean integration; as a principled, concerned, committed person; as a champion of the working class; and as an advocate of self-sufficiency. Concluding with a rationale for emphasizing the Bradshawian synthesis as a strategy of progress in the Caribbean, the author gives a real insight into the contributions of Robert Llewellyn Bradshaw, the first Premier of St. Kitts-Nevis.

223 **Youth parliaments: a parliamentary approach to the critical population problem.**
Billie Milles.   *Parliamentarian*, vol. 73, no. 4 (October 1992), p. 244-46.

Population issues and programmes are assessed by young people in national youth parliaments in ten Caribbean islands. Involving young people in this way proves beneficial for family planning, curbing adolescent fertility and promoting parliamentary democracy.

Statesman's yearbook, 1993-94.
See item no. 15.

The world factbook.
See item no. 17.

Foreign Affairs

Regional

224 **Let all ideas contend: a framework for the participation of the West Indian people in the work of the West Indian Commission.**
The West Indian Secretariat.   St. James, Barbados: The West Indian Commission, 1990. 28p.

This important document is clearly set out in brief and comprehensible chapters which describe: the setting for the West Indian Commission; the mandate of the Commission; the members of the Commission; issues for consideration; strategy and work-plan; the timetable for the Commission's work; a schedule of visits; an invitation for submission of views; and how to submit evidence. Appendix A is a communication to the people of the Caribbean Community from the West Indian Commission and Appendix B is 'Goals of the Treaty of Chaguaramas'.

225 **Much better than what we've got.**
Earl Huntley.   Bridgetown, Barbados: EC News, 1987. 5p.

Earl Huntley presents an alternative form of political union for the OECS. He describes the unique characteristics of the integration process in the Eastern Caribbean, which led to the strengthening of the collective decision-making system, and proposes a type of confederation, with regional responsibility for areas such as defence, security, foreign affairs, finance, and higher education. Although Huntley is the Permanent Secretary of Saint Lucia's Ministry of Foreign Affairs and not that of St. Kitts, the officials and people of St. Kitts-Nevis will be very interested in his views on the regional integration debate.

226 **Organisation of Eastern Caribbean States: OECS in perspective.**
Edited by Ermine Spence with a message from Kennedy Simmonds.
Castries, St. Lucia: Organisation of Eastern Caribbean States (OECS),
1987. 44p.

A charming and informative issue, commemorative of the fifth anniversary of the
OECS's foundation, which highlights the purposes, objectives and activities of
the Organisation. Since its existence, the OECS has, according to Spence, 'forged a
high degree of economic and social cooperation, secured international recognition
and respect for the dynamism . . . and is in the process of influencing realistic and
meaningful integration of model significance among mini States'. The feature article
is 'The next five years' by S. Lestrade; other articles are: 'The organisation's
mission'; 'The modus operandi of the OECS integration'; 'The work of the Economic
Affairs Secretariat and the business of the Organisation'; 'Activities of the Economic
Affairs Secretariat'; 'Activities in functional cooperation'; 'Overseas missions';
'Activities in civil aviation'; 'The Eastern Caribbean Central Bank'; and 'Relations
with the Economic commission for Latin America and the Caribbean'. The work is
illustrated with photographs of officers and employees at work; the frontispiece is a
group picture of Heads of Government and Officials of the OECS at the inaugural
meeting in St. Kitts, June 1981.

227 **Peace development and security in the Caribbean.**
Anthony T. Bryan, et al. London; Basingstoke, England: Macmillan
Press, 1990. 332p. map. bibliog.

The editors present a range of possible outcomes in the areas of peace, development
and security in the Caribbean to the year 2000. Small island states, including St.
Kitts-Nevis, are dealt with in chapters eleven, thirteen, fifteen, sixteen and seventeen.
Other editors are J. E. Green and Timothy M. Shaw.

228 **Towards West Indian survival.**
William G. Demas. Bridgetown, Barbados: The West Indian
Commission, 1990. 74p.

An essay by the president of the Caribbean Development Bank, which makes
compelling reading for people who are interested in the welfare of the Caribbean. The
preface by Shridath Ramphal, of the West Indian Commission Secretariat, provides
an astute insight into the man and the work. The chapters are exciting and include
information on: the changing world environment and the West Indies; West Indian
achievements and shortcomings; the meaning of development in the West Indies; the
economic situation, advantages and opportunities; the Caribbean Community;
the strengthening of the sense of community; sporting and cultural ties; the widening
of the community; options facing the West Indies; and West Indian survival. The
paper concludes with three simple propositions to help achieve the goals of
development, identity, self-respect and interdependence with the rest of
the world in the 1990's and into the 21st century.

229 **Treaty establishing the Organisation of Eastern Caribbean States.**
Organisation of Eastern Carribean States. Castries, St. Lucia:
Organisation of Eastern Caribbean States, 1981. 48p.

This historic and important treaty consists of the Preamble, the Articles and the
Annexes. The Articles cover the following issues: membership; the purposes and

functions of the Organisation; the composition and functions of the Foreign Affairs Committee, the Defence and Security Committe and the Economic Affairs Committee; the harmonization of foreign policy; the budget; and relations with other organizations and countries. The Annexes include various Agreements and Amendments to the treaty. The seven founding member states of the organization are Antigua, Dominica, Grenada, Montserrat, St. Kitts-Nevis, St. Lucia and St. Vincent and the Grenadines.

International

230 Commonwealth Fund for Technical Cooperation aid programmes and procedures.
Commonwealth Fund for Technical Cooperation (CFTC). London: CFTC, 1990. 10p.

The structure, organization and functions of the Commonwealth Fund for Technical Cooperation (CFTC) are outlined, and examples of its technical assistance, training and industrial development programmes are given in this short paper. In conclusion, the need for trained nationals to occupy leadership positions to enable greater economic cooperation between developing countries is emphasized.

231 Diplomacy for survival: CARICOM states in a world of change.
Lloyd Searwar. Kingston, Jamaica: Friedrich Ebert Stiftung, 1991. 97p. bibliog.

A collection of articles which deal with: Caribbean economic diplomacy; changes in international relations; geopolitics in the 1990s; and the foreign policy of Jamaica and the OECS. In his article, 'Development diplomacy and the management of foreign policy by the OECS States in the 1990s and beyond', Earl Hunte emphasizes the benefits of coordinating foreign policies through CARICOM and joint overseas representation such as is practised by the OECS countries.

232 The European Community aid programme and procedure.
E. Stahn. Bridgetown, Barbados: EEC, 1990. p. 13.

In his address given at the OECS seminar, Stahn refers to the Lome Convention which usually governs the provision of trade and aid relations between the European Community and the Caribbean. The European Commission's rationale for and approach to international assistance, and their requirements for project/programme proposals, are explained. Stahn also indicates some of the problems caused by inadequately trained staff.

233 Integration of St. Christopher into the international capitalist system.
Sylvine Henry.   Kingston, Jamaica: University of the West Indies, 1984. 16p.
Sets up an historical framework in which to examine the relationship between St. Kitts and European countries. Certain events which helped to integrate countries and mechanisms are used as examples.

Constitution and Legal System

Constitution

234 **Address of the Prime Minister over ZIZ national radio and television on the fourth anniversary of independence of St. Kitts and Nevis.**
Kennedy Simmonds.   Basseterre, St. Kitts: Office of the Prime Minister, 1987. 13p.
This address delivered, on 16 September 1987, highlights the achievements of the Government since independence. They include: the establishment of diplomatic relations with other nations; the acceleration of economic diversification; the bringing of St. Kitts and Nevis closer together in a constitutional framework; the implementation of new products in tourism, agriculture and industry; the restructuring of the sugar industry; the updating of the telecommunications systems; and the publication of a national development plan. The South East Peninsular Road project is the main development project.

235 **Constitutional status of the executive.**
Kenny D. Anthony.   Castries, St. Lucia: OECS, RCA, 1991. 20p.
This work deals with the issues, offices and options relating to the power of the executive. The offices of the executive are as follows: the Head of State; Ministers; Parliamentary Secretaries; Ministers of State; the Attorney General; the Cabinet; the Leader of the Opposition; and the Secretary to the Cabinet. Issues covered include: special advisors; the control of public prosecutions; and the prerogative of mercy. The situation in various Caribbean countries (including St. Kitts-Nevis) and non-Caribbean countries is compared.

236 **National identity and secession: the case of Nevis.**
Tony Thorndike.   Curacao: Caribbean Studies Association
Conference, 1980. 17p.

The paper analyses the Nevis secession movement and discusses the major motives
for secession from St. Kitts. It looks at the structural economic imbalance of Nevis in
comparison with St. Kitts, and the history of discrimination, especially during the
Bradshaw period. It concludes that Caribbean secessionist movements are associated
with expectations of material benefit rather than with manifestations of national
identity.

237 **Saint Christopher and Nevis Constitution Order 1983.**
St. Kitts and Nevis Government.   London: Her Majesty Stationery
Office, 1983. 121p.

This order provides a new constitution for St. Kitts and Nevis 'upon its attainment of
fully responsible government within the Commonwealth'. It replaces the Saint
Christopher-Nevis-Anguilla Constitution Order 1967 and terminates the association
of St. Kitts and Nevis with the United Kingdom, as of 19 September 1983. The
framework of government is laid out in detail and a comprehensive description of the
authorities and the powers of the organs of government is outlined. The procedures of
governing are stated and some basic human rights are laid down. The main provisions
come under the following headings: fundamental rights and freedoms; the governor-
general; parliament; the executive; citizenship; and the island of Nevis. The Order
was made at the request and with the consent of the Associated State of St. Kitts and
Nevis, under section 5 (4) of the West Indies Act 1967.

238 **The similarities and differences of the constitution of St. Kitts and
Nevis and Jamaica.**
Irving R. Sweeney.   In: *Convention of Jamaican Constitution.*
Kingston, Jamaica: Bustamante Institute of Public International
Affairs, 1986, p. 34-37.

Compares and contrasts the constitution of St. Kitts with that of Jamaica under
selected areas, for example: preamble, interpretation, bill of rights, governor-general
and parliament. A major finding is that in the composition of parliament, the St. Kitts-
Nevis parliament is unicameral, having one House, while the Jamaica Parliament is
bicameral, with the lower House of Representatives and the upper House of Senate.
(The constitution of St. Kitts and Nevis came into operation on 22 June 1983 to
facilitate independence on 19 September 1983)

Legal system

239 **(Acts) Statutes of the islands of Saint Christopher and Anguilla.**
Saint Christopher Government.   Basseterre, St. Kitts: The Authority,
1857. 395p.

In addition to the Acts, there is an appendix of three Leeward Islands Acts. A table of
Acts and an index to the Acts help to make the material more accessible.

240 **Caribbean law and business.**
Velma Newton. Bridgetown, Barbados: Caribbean Law Institute,
1989. 8p.
These conference proceedings on the harmonization of shipping legislation in the
Caribbean Community cover topics such as: maritime law; the law of the sea;
territorial sea; and environmental legislation.

241 **Commonwealth Parliamentary Association: report of proceedings.**
Commonwealth Parliamentary Association. London: Commonwealth
Parliamentary Association, 1987. 64p.
Records the proceedings of a conference held at Jersey, 22-23 September 1986. The
problem of pollution and environmental damage was addressed and the need for an
all-nations insurance protection fund was discussed. The debate covered issues such
as: the parliamentary scrutiny of public spending; the financial security of small
states; the social and economic implications of drugs; and the future of parliamentary
democracy.

242 **Insuring foreign risks: St. Kitts-Nevis.**
In: *Insuring foreign risks: a guide to regulations world-wide.* Edited by
G. N. Gockford. Kingston-upon-Thames, England: Kluwer Publishing,
1993. 2p.
Forms part of a loose-leaf publication aimed at providing the basic facts about 'the
way in which [each] country regulates insurance . . . a reflection of its history,
political system and social organisation'. For St. Kitts-Nevis, it comments briefly on
the following topics, amongst others: insurance legislation, the formation and
operations of insurance companies, state involvement in insurance, premium taxes
and levies, insurance and contract law, etc. Updates are published periodically

243 **Laws of St. Kitts-Nevis and Anguilla.**
Basseterre, St. Kitts: Government of St. Kitts-Nevis and Anguilla,
1958.
This series consists of bound, annual volumes up to 1970. The series is useful for
retrospective and comparative study of law, on the local, regional or international
level. Current laws are now contained in the *Official Gazette.*

244 **Laws of the West Indies.**
West Indian Federation. Port of Spain, Trinidad: West Indian
Federation, 1958.
Some legislation made by this Federal Body during 1958-62 is still in force and is
applicable to St. Kitts-Nevis.

245 **Revised laws of St. Christopher, Nevis and Anguilla**.
P. Cecil Lewis. London: St. Christopher-Nevis-Anguilla
Government, 1964. rev. ed. 8 vols.
This set contains the laws in force in the country on 24 October 1961.

246 **Saint Christopher and Nevis consolidated index of statutes and subsidiary legislation to 1st January 1991.**
Faculty of Law Library, University of the West Indies.   Cave Hill, Barbados: Faculty of Law of the University of the West Indies, 1991. 8 vols.

An index to the laws of Saint Christopher and Nevis, arranged by title and reference number. The laws referred to in the index are: statutes and subsidiary legislation in force on 24 October 1961, contained in volumes 1 to 8 of the 1961 revised edition of *Laws of St. Christopher, Nevis and Anguilla*; statutes enacted and statutory rules and orders made between 24 October 1961 and 31 December 1990; federal laws continued in force after the dissolution of the West Indian Federation and adaptations; and some of the United Kingdom Statutes and Statutory Instruments which are in force in the state or which are relevant to laws in force in the state.

247 **St. Christopher and Nevis Legislative Council Standing Rules and Orders and the St. Christopher-Nevis Act 1882.**
St. Christopher and Nevis Legislature.   Basseterre, St. Kitts: The Author, 1882. 18p.

These are the Orders regulating the business of the Legislature which remain relevant today.

248 **Saint Christopher and Nevis Official Gazette.**
Basseterre, St. Kitts: The Authority, 1905.

Contains current legislation, ordinances, regulations and irregular supplements of High Court decisions. Earlier Court reports can be found in *West Indian Reports* (London: Butterworths, 1960). The *Gazette* supersedes the *St. Kitts-Nevis-Anguilla Official Gazette* from 1981.

249 **St. Kitts-Nevis Bar Association.**
Theodore Hobson.   Basseterre, St. Kitts: St. Kitts-Nevis Bar Association Council, 1992. 4p.

Records the report for the year 1991-92. Activities of that year are reviewed, for example: representation on various forums, including the OECS Bar Association; the Company Law Institute; and the Council of Legal Education. Another development is the appointment of a Legislative Committee whose function is to advise on and examine Government Bills and Legislative proposals from the Caribbean Law Institute, and to initiate law reform where necessary. The adoption of the OECS Code of ethics and the Association's new draft Constitution should provide the mechanism needed to deal with discipline, integrity and sanctions. Radio programmes introduced to promote the Association are 'the Law and you' and 'aspects of the Law', a fifteen-minute weekly talk.

250 **St. Kitts-Nevis: description of national legislation relating to natural resources management.**
Barbara Lausche.   Castries, St. Lucia: OECS Natural Resources
Management Project, 1986. 14p.

Lausche lists relevant legislation pertaining to land, including: planning and development agriculture; forests; water; tourism; industry; beaches; protected areas; wildlife; and waste management. The effects of existing laws are analysed and those sectors requiring urgent attention are identified.

251 **St. Kitts-Nevis (Laws).**
Thomas H. Reynolds.   In: *Foreign law: current sources of codes and basic legislation in Jurisdictions of the World, vol. 1. – The Western Hemisphere (Latin America and Canada).*   Thomas H. Reynolds, Arturo A. Flures.   Littleton, Colorado: Fred B. Rothman & Co., 1989, p. 1-16.

The introduction provides an historical background to the legal structure and court system of St. Kitts-Nevis, and lists the major publications containing translations, digests or outlines of legislation. The main body of the contribution is arranged by subject headings and covers every aspect of the law, from administrative law, procedure, and bankruptcy to company law, environmental protection, and workers' compensation. Under each heading, there is an alphabetical listing of relevant acts with dates, and occasional explanatory notes where the authors deem it helpful. Compiled by two American law librarians, the work is massive, and provides a useful tool for the reference of librarians, lawyers and lay people. It is in the AALL Publ Series no. 33 and was sponsored by the American Association of Law Libraries.

The Caribean: selected maritime law and policy issues.
See item no. 375.

Implications of the new Law of the Sea Convention for the Eastern Caribbean.
See item no. 380.

Administration and
Local Government

252 Dialogue.
Charlestown, Nevis: Nevis Island Administration, 1984-   . monthly.
Records and reviews events which take place in Nevis, for instance: the holding of
local elections; the swearing in of a newly elected government; the government's
policy statement; commissioning; and presentations.

253 Speech from the throne.
Clement Arrindell.   *Labour Spokesman*, vol. 35, no. 27
(15 August 1992), p. 10-11.
An index of the Nevis Administration's goals, plans and policies for 1992. Sectors
targeted for new policies are: tourism; agriculture; infrastructure; utilities; education;
health; youth; women; and community development. The Governor-General
concludes 'the implementation of these policies requires the strictest adherence to the
dictates of fiscal prudence'. The 'speech' is an annual occurence, and its content
could be a useful measure by which to compare the island's growth and progress.

Statistics

254 Annual digest of statistics for 1982.
Basseterre, St. Kitts: St. Kitts-Nevis Planning Unit, 1983.

Presents the country's economic and social performance for 1982, in statistical form.
It also includes statistics for population, education, labour and employment, transport
and communication, tourism, trade, public finance and the gross national product.

255 Caribbean Tourism Statistical Report.
Christ Church, Barbados: Caribbean Tourism Research and
Development Centre, 1978- . annual.

Tourism activity in the region and in individual islands is presented in numerous
tables and graphs of statistical data, which include the following information: the
number of hotels and their ratings; the number of rooms; the number of tourists
entering; their countries of origin; and the length of their stay. It is useful for a
comparative, regional study on tourism.

256 Report on the re-organisation of the statistical system in St. Kitts-Nevis.
W. Chinnia.   Basseterre, St. Kitts: United Nations Statistical Office;
OECS, 1981. 56p.

The results of an investigation into the government statistical system are presented
here in nine sections: the evaluation of the current system; minimum statistical
programme; structure; the organization and functions of a central Statistical Office;
job descriptions (four sections); and recommendations.

257 Statistical digest 1989: Nevis.
Charlestown, Nevis: Nevis Administration, 1990.

This compendium of statistics covers a five-year period from 1985-89. Statistics are
tabulated under the following headings: climate; population and vital statistics;

housing; education; medical and health; leisure; tourism; transport and communication; trade; agricultural production; finance; local revenue; other recurrent revenue; and capital revenue. Under leisure, Table 6.1 shows the number of radio stations, television stations, public libraries, and books in circulation. In addition to the statistical tables, there is a foreword, explanatory notes, and general information.

258 Statistical survey of St. Kitts-Nevis.
In: *Europa yearbook 1994*. London: Europa Publications Ltd, 1994, p. 2525-29.

Statistics recorded relate to: areas and population; agriculture; industry; finance; external trade; transport; education; constitution; political organizations; the judicial system; religion; the press; radio and television; and trade and industry. Raw sugar exported in 1992 amounted to 20,159 metric tons. It constitutes an authoritative source for up-to-date figures and information.

259 Statistical yearbook 1989.
UNESCO. Paris: UNESCO, 1990.

The world's statistics are tabulated under headings such as: education; literacy; culture and communication; libraries; and science and technology. The St. Kitts section records under education that there are thirty-six pre-primary (1985) schools, forty-six teachers and 1,501 pupils. The *UN Monthly Bulletin of Statistics* is a more up-to-date source because of its frequency of publication.

260 Statistics in brief 1981-88.
Basseterre, St. Kitts: St. Kitts-Nevis Planning Unit, 1988. 22p.

A consolidated record of eight years of statistics. Data is given on: climate and land area; demography; employment and social security; education; health; transport and communication; housing; travel and tourism; banking and finance; agriculture and industry; retail prices; international trade; economic aggregates and other economic indicators.

Europa world yearbook.
See item no. 8.

The world factbook.
See item no. 17.

Population census of the Commonwealth Caribbean, 1980-1981.
See item no. 124.

Caribbean Economic Almanac.
See item no. 517.

Annual digest of statistics.
See item no. 549.

Economy

General and regional

261   **The Caribbean: challenges for economic development.**
Anthony Layng.   New York: Elmira College, 1989.
This paper results from an America Partnership Development Workshop, convened
on 5 March 1988, and highlights common social and historical traditions of the
Caribbean. Racial complexity and geographical diversity are analysed, cultural
commonality with shared heritage and problems are surfaced. Also relevant is Simon
Jones-Hendrickson's article, 'Factors constraining growth of Microstate economies'
in *Proceedings of the Conference of Environmental Management and Economic
growth in smaller Caribbean islands*, edited by William Beller (Washington, DC:
Department of State Publications 8996, International Organisation and Conference
Series 143, 1979, p. 31-41).

262   **Caricom in review: a macro-economic profile.**
Caribbean Contact, vol. 20, no. 1 (January-Febuary 1994), p. 12-14.
Sourced from Sir Neville Nicholls's (President of the Caribbean Development Bank)
review of the economic performance of the Bank and its borrowing member
countries, and his preview of the prospects for Caribbean countries, this report
analyses the macro-economic performance of the countries of the Caribbean
Community (CARICOM). It gives the general picture, covering: borrowing and
output; tourism; bananas; sugar; petroleum; bauxite; and the medium-term prospects
of projects. St. Kitts-Nevis is among the 'relatively strong performers' in relation to
real output growth in 1993. The analysis also finds that sugar production in St. Kitts-
Nevis was estimated to have performed comparatively well, following the devastation
of the fields during Hurricane Hugo in 1989. 'Export values improved and earnings
were projected to remain relatively steady . . . as the U.S. quota for St. Kitts-Nevis
sugar was not reduced along with the rest of the Caribbean region'.

263 **Historical perspective of OECS economic integration over the past ten years.**
Carlyle Mitchell. St. John's, Antigua: Organisation of Eastern Caribbean States, 1992. 15p.
The theoretical bases for integration and development, and the objectives and functions of the OECS Secretariats for regional integration are examined. Integration developments are traced from 1982-1991 and the impact and growth in the region is assessed.

264 **An introduction to property investment in St. Kitts-Nevis.**
St. Kitts-Nevis Tourist Board. In: *St. Kitts-Nevis Tourist Guide.* St. Kitts-Nevis Tourist Board. St. Johns, Antigua: FT International, 1983, p. 14-16.
A detailed account of current major development projects in St. Kitts-Nevis, for example, the Frigate Bay development in St. Kitts. The article also points to opportunities for investment, giving incentives to developers.

265 **Investment, trade and finance**.
Delisle Worrell. Basseterre, St. Kitts: Commonwealth Secretariat, Eastern Caribbean Central Bank, 1991. 9p.
Worrell deals specifically with small states, including St. Kitts-Nevis, and with the Caribbean generally in this short work. He comments on policies that should promote growth in small economies and discusses these policies with respect to investment, trade and finance. He covers areas such as: devaluation; foreign exchange reserves; trade policy; export promotion; and credit. This paper was given at the 'Symposium on small states: problems and opportunities in a world of rapid change', which was held at Basseterre in March 1991.

266 **A look at property on St. Kitts-Nevis.**
St. Kitts-Nevis Tourist Board. In: *St. Kitts-Nevis Tourist Guide.* St. Kitts-Nevis Tourist Board. St. Johns, Antigua: FT International, 1984, p. 11, 14.
This article shows existing opportunities in the property market, covering residential house lots, already completed houses, and fully furnished condominiums. It also includes information regarding costs, financing and incentives.

267 **Luncheon address to the Caribbean Association of Industry and Commerce.**
Kennedy A. Simmonds. Basseterre, St. Kitts: [n.p.], 1984. 13p.
Delivered on 10 May 1984, this address evaluates the industrial development of St. Kitts-Nevis, showing the success of the private and public sectors venture and suggesting that industry and commerce could be a potential source of government revenue. Government developments include a comprehensive programme of training, utilizing the private sector. Simmonds assesses the effectiveness of CARICOM with reference to problems in intra-regional trade, access to markets, stringent licensing policies and problems of currency fluctuation.

268 **The Organisation of Eastern Caribbean States (OECS) small business sector: a strategy for development.**
Chambre de Metiers. St. John's, Antigua: Organisation of Eastern Caribbean States, Eastern Associated States, 1992. 96p.
An overview of the economies of the OECS with a special emphasis on the small business sector. After examining the infrastructure – institutional support, training, technical assistance, financial services and credit as required by small businesses – de Metiers recommends a strategy and action plan to develop the small business sector in OECS countries.

269 **Post-war economic development of St. Kitts.**
Sylvine Henry. Kingston, Jamaica: 1983. 39p.
The author identifies the effects of the international capitalist system on the economic development of St. Kitts. He covers the period 1945-83, subdivided by political status, assesses economic development from 1980-83 and offers recommendations.

270 **St. Christopher and Nevis: updating economic memorandum.**
Washington, DC: International Bank for Reconstruction and Development, 1986. 55p.
A review of economic developments and principal policy issues for St. Kitts and Nevis for the previous year. Some areas covered are: public sector financing; the balance of payments; external debt; an input-output analysis; investment policy; statistical analysis; and macroeconomics.

271 **St. Kitts and Nevis: problems of economic development.**
Keith Glasgow. Basseterre, St. Kitts: St. Kitts and Nevis Teachers Training College, [n.d.]. 26p.
Glasgow gives several reasons for the slow pace of economic development in St. Kitts-Nevis. Conclusions are drawn from the data collected, and some recommendations are offered.

272 **Sustainable development and foreign investment in the Eastern Caribbean: a strategy for the 1990s and beyond.**
Benjamin Goss, Dennis Conway. *Bulletin of Latin American Research*, vol. 11, no. 3 (September 1992), p. 307-26. bibliog.
With particular reference to the Eastern Caribbean states, including St. Kitts-Nevis, the authors focus on export-oriented industrialization catalysed by direct foreign investment in manufacturing, as one path which these small islands are following in the interest of their development goals. Useful tables of statistics are provided.

Development plans

273 **National development plan of St. Kitts and Nevis 1986-1990.**
Basseterre, St. Kitts: Ministry of Agriculture, Lands, Housing and
Development, 1986. vi, 236p.

Reviews the economy of St. Kitts-Nevis over a period of five years (1986-90), and
outlines: national economic and trade policy; sectoral plans and programmes in
agriculture; industry and tourism; public utilities; transport and communication;
housing; health; national security; human resource development; and public sector
investment.

274 **Nevis development plan, 1987-1991.**
Charlestown, Nevis: Ministry of Development and Planning, 1990.
70p. map.

A five year development plan for Nevis presented in seven sections as follows:
general background and review of the economy; macroeconomic and foreign trade
policy; sector plans and programmes; infrastructure and social services; human
resource and manpower development; off-shore companies; and the financing of the
plan. Appendix A provides a list of public sector projects.

275 **Saint Christopher and Nevis.**
John Mckensie.   Charlestown, Nevis: Nevis Island Administration,
1990. 35p.

The potential business opportunities of Nevis are analysed. Mckensie examines the
potential of various sectors such as farming, fishing, transport, food preparation,
construction, manufacturing, services and distributive trades. The constraints which
are associated with the growth of small and medium enterprises in terms of
institutional, financial, technical, managerial, educational and marketing aspects are
also discussed.

Investment

276 **Investors' information.**
Basseterre, St. Kitts: St. Kitts-Nevis Investment Promotion Agency,
[n.d.]. 14p.

A useful document for potential investors in the islands. It explains how a business
may be established and gives information on: electricity and water rates; telephone
service and rates; banking; lawyers; building contractors; construction costs; real
estate agents and developers; insurance companies; couriers; minimum rates; port
charges; sea cargo container services; and air cargo services.

277 **Investors' information.**
Basseterre, St. Kitts: St. Kitts-Nevis Investment Promotion Agency, 1987. 7p.

Provides further useful information for investors and covers: Federal Government leaders; labour unions; communications and transportation; shipping agents; business information; foreign investors operating in St. Kitts-Nevis; tourist information; and the general economic situation of the nation.

278 **Review of the activities of the Investment Promotion Agency of St. Christopher-Nevis (IPA).**
Kenrick Clifton.   Basseterre, St. Kitts: Investment Promotion Agency of St. Christopher-Nevis (IPA), 1990. 20p.

The role of the IPA and the background to government policy are outlined. The changing role from promoting foreign investment to an industrial development agency is stressed and the achievements of the IPA for the year ending 31 December 1989 are detailed.

Optimun size and nature of new hotel development in the Caribbean.
See item no. 65.

Agricultural development in Nevis.
See item no. 307.

Experiences in agricultural diversification in St. Kitts.
See item no. 316.

St. Kitts-Nevis country environmental profile.
See item no. 364.

The Southeast Peninsular project in St. Kitts.
See item no. 365.

Caribbean Insight.
See item no. 520.

Finance, Tax, Banking and Currency

279 **Budget address 1990.**
Kennedy A. Simmonds. Basseterre, St. Kitts: Ministry of Finance, 1989. 52p.

The introduction speaks of the political, economic and social life of St. Kitts-Nevis over the last decade. It states the mission, goals and objectives of the Government, and discusses the following topics: international economy; economic developments and trends; fiscal prospects; tourism; and industry. The heart of the speech reviews the performances of the economy and outlines projects for 1990. Up-to-date budget speeches are available from the Ministry.

280 **Deepening financial management in the Organisation of Eastern Caribbean Countries (OECS).**
S. Jones-Hendrickson. St. Thomas, US Virgin Islands: University of the Virgin Islands, 1990. 14p. bibliog.

Explores the underpinning of the key issues of financial management in the OECS. It focuses and advises on: strategic planning; factor mobility – capital and labour; Regional Central Bank; and common currency. The author defines financial management as 'the conscious manipulation of public sector revenues and expenditures in a directed, controlled manner, such that specific planned goals and objectives are attained'. Jones-Hendrickson is a professor of economics at the University of the Virgin Islands and the paper was prepared for the Regional Programme of Monetary Studies, Georgetown, Guyana, 15-19 October 1990. Other related articles by the author are: 'Financial structure and economic development in the OECS' in *Social and Economic Studies* (q.v.), and *The gradation policy of the World Bank International Development Agency as it affects the OECS and other small states in the Commonwealth* (St. John's, Antigua: Commonwealth Secretariat, Organisation of East Caribbean States, 1985. 83p.).

281 **The disassociation factor in revenue production – St. Kitts-Nevis-Anguilla.**
S. B. Jones-Hendrickson. *Social and Economic Studies*, vol 27, no. 3 (1978), p. 237-55.

The author defines the 'disassociation factor' as a concept characterizing the unexplained factor of growth in public expenditure. The introduction is followed by a normative, macroeconomic model with solutions for the instrument variables. Section three offers a dynamic model from which the empirical equations are obtained, followed by partial data for St. Kitts-Nevis-Anguilla, giving regression, results and analysis. The fifth section deals with revenue, growth, production functions and the disassociation factor. The conclusion summarizes the public finance rationale which underlies this analysis.

282 **The Eastern Caribbean Central Bank marks its tenth anniversary.**
Basseterre, St. Kitts: Eastern Caribbean Central Bank, 1993.

This press release announces the tenth anniversary of the Bank, which commenced operations from its headquarters in Basseterre, St. Kitts. It gives the historical background of the Bank and highlights its additional responsibilities in an attempt to heighten public awareness about its role and services. Some of its responsibilities are: to promote monetary stability; to establish a sound financial structure; and to further the economic development of member states. The issue of a revised edition of the booklet entitled 'The Eastern Caribbean Central Bank; its role and functions in the Financial system', first published in 1983, was one of the activities celebrating a decade of service.

283 **Exchange rate development.**
Basseterre, St. Kitts: Eastern Caribbean Currency Bank, 1986. 9p.

Covers public finance, prices and wages in OECS countries (including St. Kitts-Nevis), the background and current status of the exchange rate, and the work of the Bank.

284 **Financial structure and economic development in the OECS.**
Simon Jones-Hendrickson. *Social and Economic Studies*, vol. 38, no. 4 (1989), p. 71-93.

Hendrickson examines the link between financial structure and economic development in seven countries of the OECS, St. Kitts-Nevis being one of them. The analysis is 'Ekistic' – conducted with the basic needs of the individual state in mind, using the entire community as a frame of reference. The various systems and doctrines which support the arguments are featured, for example: economic development; the interaction of society and government; direct and indirect taxes; subsidies; revenue; and loans and grants. Several tables and graphs help to clarify the points raised. Table one indicates that the highest indirect tax of St. Kitts in 1987 was 35.4 per cent; and the highest direct tax in 1985 was 36.8 per cent.

285 **Foreign aid, debt and technical assistance in small open economies: the ECCB case.**
Arthur Williams, Wayne Mitchell, John Venner.   Basseterre, St. Kitts: Commonwealth Secretariat, Eastern Caribbean Central Bank, 1991. 13p.
This paper claims that despite the fragility, structural weaknesses and vulnerability of the economies of the Eastern Caribbean Central Bank region, these economies grew significantly (in real terms) during the 1980s. Table one shows the structural composition of GNP for 1989, and indicates the following situation in St. Kitts: agriculture 8.9; manufactures 10.6; hotels 5.8; transportation 16.9; financial services 10.7; and government 18.9. However, the growth in the leading sectors has artificially inflated per capita income, and has presented an exaggerated picture of the standard of living and the ability of the economies to sustain growth.

286 **Guidelines for negotiation of double tax treaties and tax information agreements for the OECS States.**
Claude H. Denbow.   New York: United Nations Centre on Transnational Corporations, 1990. 42p.
Examines existing Double Taxation treaties between OECS countries and developed countries in relation to the treatment of transfer payments, covering royalties, dividends, profits, interest and management charges. Denbow also scrutinizes provisions designed to counteract those practices of multinational corporations which aim to extract profit in non-taxable forms, and provides recommendations on the harmonization and upgrading of relevant OECS tax laws.

287 **Public finance and monetary policy in open economies.**
Simon Jones-Hendrickson.   Kingston, Jamaica: Institute of Social and Economic Research, 1985. 172p. bibliog.
In this valuable and original work, Jones-Hendrickson treats the integration of fiscal and monetary policy in open economies in a systematic way. He addresses the inadequacies which exist between and among classes in the Third World economic systems and lays special emphasis on the Commonwealth Caribbean, including St. Kitts-Nevis where he was born. Among the topics discussed are: the integrative nature of public finance and monetary policies; positive and normative views; and a rationale for an integrative fiscal and monetary policy for the Caribbean. Other relevant works by this author are: *The gradation policy of the World Bank International Development Agency as it affects the Organisation of Eastern Caribbean States (OECS) and the smaller states in the Commonwealth.* (London: Commonwealth Secretariat, 1985), and *Report of the Committee to examine the role of the Eastern Caribbean Common Market (ECCM) Sub-regional Integration Movement* (St. Johns, Antigua: ECCM Secretariat, 1980).

288 **Readings in Caribbean public sector economics.**
Edited by Fuat Andic, Simon Jones-Hendrickson, foreword by A. R. Prest.   Kingston, Jamaica: Institute of Social and Economic Research, 1981. 290p. bibliog.
These essays, which relate to the Caribbean and the Third World, are presented by internationally renowned experts and scholars in the field of public finance and taxation. The work is concerned with public sector finance in small economies, and

studies various problems encountered in financing and in public administration. Chapter ten in section four deals specifically with St. Kitts.

289 Recent debt and adjustment in OECS countries of the Caribbean.
Jerome L. McElroy, Klaus De Albuquerque. *Caribbean Affairs*, vol. 3, no. 1. [n.d.], p. 57-64.

The authors review the experiences of seven OECS countries (including St. Kitts-Nevis) and reveal 'a rapid build-up in debt primarily on concessional terms during the past decade, a time-frame coinciding with the restructuring of traditional plantation economy toward tourism and export manufacturing, a period also characterised by a migration reversal and rising insular population densities'. The case of St. Kitts-Nevis is used to illustrate three related issues: the strategic impact of export revenues on domestic finances; the intense competition for fiscal resources in microstates which are undergoing restructuring; and the precarious nature of credit worthiness even for a low-debt country with no arrears when natural disaster strikes. The article concludes with the 'relevancy of traditional IMF medicine – budget, real wage, and currency cuts – for such dependent countries in the throes of payment difficulties, and whether a more appropriate kind of conditionality can be formulated for such societies engaged in restructuring and transformation'. There are four useful tables which cover the following: recent performance indicators; external public debt outstanding; debt outstanding to GNP in percentages; and debt service to merchandise exports and nonfactor services.

290 Reflections on the World Bank commentary on the Eastern Currency Authority.
George Theophilus. Basseterre, St. Kitts: Eastern Caribbean Currency Authority, 1977. 35p.

Deals with the workings of the three following institutions as they affect OECS countries and price stabilization: the Eastern Caribbean Currency Bank; the Eastern Caribbean Currency Authority; and the World Bank.

291 St. Kitts-Nevis-Anguilla National Bank Ltd Report.
Church Street, St. Kitts: St. Kitts-Nevis Anguilla National Bank Ltd. annual.

A summary of the annual activity and detailed accounts of the St. Kitts-Nevis-Anguilla National Bank Ltd. and its subsidiaries.

292 The tax structure of the Organisation of Eastern Caribbean countries.
Laurel Bain. *Bulletin of Eastern Caribbean Affairs*, vol. 16, no. 6 (January-February 1991), p. 27-40.

The tax structure of OECS countries, including St. Kitts-Nevis, is examined for the period 1977-88. Several types of taxes, including corporate tax, consumption taxes and duties, value added tax, and personal tax, are compared and contrasted.

Trade and Industry

293 Cane fires on a British West Indian island.
Nathaniel Raymond. *Social and Economic Studies*, vol. 16 (1967), p. 280-88.

A discussion outlining the factors which caused the cane fires in St. Kitts during 1961. Possible causes are deemed to be: the shortage of labour; changing work patterns; overgrown fields; and labour relations.

294 The Caribbean after 1992.
Alister McIntyre. *RSA Journal*, no. 138 (November 1990), p. 816-25.

Discusses the effects of the Single European Market on the Caribbean and touches on factors such as trade and development, external financing and human resources.

295 Critical look at the human resource in the sugar industry – the monoculture economy of St. Kitts.
Valerie Liburd. Basseterre, St. Kitts: St. Kitts and Nevis Teachers Training College, [n.d.]. 28p.

Liburd deals here with the relationships between specific groups of persons directly involved with the operation of the sugar industry – the government, the opposition and the sugar-workers. She offers recommendations, and urges the various groups to make sacrifices for the benefit of the industry and of society.

296 Feasibility study for a molasses ethanol distillery in Basseterre.
Washington, DC: Organisation of American States, 1986. iii, 112p.

Presents the findings of a feasibility study for the production of ethanol from Blackstrap molasses in Basseterre.

297 **Great Salt Pond development, St. Kitts, West Indies.**
Basseterre, St. Kitts: Beard Dove Caribbean, 1981. map.
The costing of the Great Salt Pond development project is detailed in this preliminary report.

298 **Integration of agriculture and tourism.**
Lawrence Lewis. Basseterre, St. Kitts: [n.p.], 1984. 9p.
Lewis debates the possibility of St. Kitt's successfully blending tourism and agriculture. He outlines the different types of tourist who visit the island, and explains the importance of increased investment in tourism. Guidelines and recommendations to ensure success in this area are presented, one being that some of the sugar lands should be converted for other production crops, which are required for hotel consumption and harvest storability. Self sufficiency, with the ability to supply hotels with vegetables, should be a primary aim.

299 **Monocrop economy: agricultural analysis of St. Kitts' sugar industry.**
Douglas D. Wattley. Basseterre, St. Kitts: St. Kitts and Nevis Teachers Training College, [n.d.]. 26p.
The sugar production industry of St. Kitts is examined with an emphasis on fluctuation and the costs of production. Wattley also touches upon the problems encountered in the industry, their possible causes, and the effects of a declining industry on society, and offers some solutions.

300 **Review of the construction sector in St. Kitts.**
Peter R. A. Jenkins. Port of Spain, Trinidad: University of the West Indies, 1984. 191p.
Consisting of three parts, this report examines factors which affect the construction sector and offers suggestions to improve efficiency and capacity, for example, improved financing and the reduction of the cost of materials and components.

301 **St. Christopher and Nevis external trade report: summary tables 1983.**
Ministry of Agriculture, Lands, Housing and Development.
Basseterre, St. Kitts: Planning Unit, 1984. v, 34p.
Based on the standard trade classification issued by the United Nations Economic and Social Council, this summary of trade information is compiled from Customs Warrants covering the past year. Up-to-date reports are available from the Ministry.

302 **St. Kitts' salt industry.**
New Commonwealth, (February 1951), p. 350-51.
Several plates help to illustrate the working of salt ponds on the estate of Dr. Arthur Wilkin. In 1951, 65,000 barrels were reaped and exported mainly to Guiana, Trinidad and Barbados, and 400 people were employed in 'reaping'.

303 **The Single European market of 1992: implications and policy options for Caribbean agriculture.**
Dowlat Budhram, Lorenzo Rock. San Jose, Costa Rica: Inter-American Institute for Cooperation in Agriculture (IICA), 1991. 116p.

Budhram outlines the agricultural trade policies of the Single European Market. Monetary and economic policies are defined and Caribbean economic aspects in the light of marketing in European communities are highlighted. The work also offers suggestions for crop diversification in the Caribbean in order to compete in the European market.

304 **A single market in the Organisation of Eastern Caribbean States (OECS).**
Carlyle L. Mitchell. Basseterre, St. Kitts: Eastern Caribbean Central Bank, 1991. 13p.

The degree of economic integration attained by the OECS and the measures necessary for the creation of a single OECS market are described by Mitchell in this short paper. The economic implications of such a market are also examined by the author, who touches on related factors such as: customs unions; legislation; tax exemptions; tariffs; migration law; private enterprises; and the public sector.

305 **Sugar industry of St. Kitts and Nevis: the post war experience.**
Sonita Barrett. Mona, Jamaica: University of the West Indies, 1985. 87p.

The performance of the economy with reference to the sugar industry in St. Kitts and Nevis is considered. Barrett offers an economic profile, a description of the sugar industry, and an outline of its history and structural development, and discusses its contribution to the national output. This study, a BA thesis, concludes with an analysis and several recommendations.

306 **Trade policies and prospects**.
Jack I. Stone. New York: United Nations, Technical Centre for Agricultural and Rural Co-operation (CTA), Organisation of Eastern Caribbean States (OECS), 1990. 60p.

In this publication, Stone draws economical and cultural comparisons between the OECS and the French Overseas Departments (DFA). He goes on to review the structures of the DFA trade, by export products and by countries exporting, and the intra-trade of the OECS and DFAs. Economic, legal and cultural constraints, non-tariff barriers to trade, and investment between the two groups are noted, as are governmental levels towards promoting further regional cooperation. The work is the first volume of the publication *Aid and investment relations between the Member States of the Organisation Of Eastern Caribbean States (OECS) and the French Overseas Departments (DFAs) in the Caribbean.*

Caribbean Update.
See item no. 529.

Agriculture

General and regional

307 **Agricultural development in Nevis: implementation of development programme, vol 1.**
I. R. Gordon. Surrey, England: Overseas Development Administration, 1984. viii, 9p. (Series no. 141).
Presents a summary of constraints to agricultural development, for example: soil type; low fertility; seasonal variations in rainfall; and crop damage due to the uncontrolled grazing of animals. Stated development objectives are: the reduction of imports; additional employment opportunities; the reduction of soil erosion; and the provision of new farms for settlement. An outline of the CARDI programme on the island of Nevis is also presented.

308 **Agricultural development in Nevis: development proposals for government estates, vol 2.**
K. Davies, M. Springton, I. R. Gordon. Surrey, England: Overseas Development Administration, 1984. v, 79p. bibliog.
Project proposals are presented under the following subheadings: background, proposals and project costs. These projects include the development of water resources, the establishment of a landuse unit in the Department of Agriculture, the improvement of farm machinery, the establishment of an animal feed production unit, the production of animal feed and raw materials for animal feed mills, and the Cades Bay irrigation crop/citrus production schemes. Information on the agricultural sector and on government estates is provided as are financial and economic analyses of development proposals. Also underlined is the interdependence of some components of the development programme.

309 **Agricultural development in Nevis: appendixes, vol 3.**
K. Davies, M. Springton, I. R. Gordon.   Surrey, England: Overseas
Development Administration, 1984.

There are eleven appendixes under the following headings: ground water drilling
project; pilot irrigation project; Spring Hill / Cades Bay irrigation project; tick
eradication programme; establishment of an abattoir; inputs supply revolving fund;
small farms equipment pool; pasture improvement methods; upgrading of oil
extraction plant; agricultural holdings in Nevis; and crop budgets. Each heading is
discussed, and accompanied by conclusions and recommendations.

310 **Agricultural policy and collective self-reliance in the Caribbean.**
W. Andrew Axline.   Boulder, Colorado; London: Westview Press,
1986. 127p. bibliog.

A descriptive analysis of the adoption of regional agricultural policies among the
states that constitute the Caribbean Community and Common Market (CARICOM).
The introduction provides the background to Caribbean integration, and offers
summaries of how each of the six chapters is treated. There are twelve tables which
help to clarify text and thesis.

311 **Agricultural problems of small states with special reference to
Commonwealth Caribbean countries.**
B. Persaud.   London: Commonwealth Secretariat, 1987. 16p.

Persaud outlines agricultural problems in small states and touches on some solutions
in order to maximise the agricultural potential of the territories. The paper was
presented at a symposium on the economic development and prospects of the OECS
states.

312 **Crop diversification in St. Kitts.**
Conrad Kelly.   Basseterre, St. Kitts: National Agricultural
Corporation, 1982. 12p.

Prefaced by an historical review, the work presents a survey of crop diversification on
St. Kitts and supports the Government's policies in this area. It outlines production
constraints and recommends the carrying out of a detailed land use survey.

313 **Cropping systems in the tropics.**
Shirley Evelyn.   St. Augustine, Trinidad: University of the West
Indies, 1989. 64p.

Evelyn, a University librarian, is an expert in Caribbean bibliography and has
compiled several subject bibliographies over the years. This is a list of references to
cropping systems carried out in the tropics and cited in the Caribbean Agricultural
Information System database for the period 1980-88. It will enable agriculturalists to
familiarize themselves with developments in the field, and will help them to avoid
unnecessary duplication of effort, research and experiment in individual agricultural
departments throughout the region.

314 **A digest of Organisation of Eastern Caribbean States (OECS) non-traditional agricultural exports (1988-1990): volume 2.**
Organisation of Eastern Caribbean States, Agricultural Diversification Co-ordination Unit, US Agency for International Development. Washington, DC: Sibley International, 1992. 140p.

This publication provides export data (volume and value) for non-traditional crops, such as: breadfruit, dasheen/eddoes, hot peppers, melons, mangoes, plantains, pumpkin, sweet potatoes and avocados. An overall summary for the OECS is given as well as data for individual countries, including St. Kitts-Nevis.

315 **Edible fruits and vegetables of the English-speaking Caribbean.**
Devi P. V. Prasad. Kingston, Jamaica: Caribbean Food and Nutrition Institute, Pan American Health Organisation/World Health Organization, 1986. 68p.

This text, which is well illustrated with pictures, tables and diagrams, describes Caribbean fruits and vegetables, giving their nutritional value as well. It is a useful guide for students, dietitians, agriculturalists and farmers.

316 **Experiences in agricultural diversification in St. Kitts.**
C. Kelly. In: *Agricultural diversification in the Caribbean: CARDI, CTA Proceedings 27 Nov – 1 December 1989.* Bridgetown, Barbados: Technical Centre for Agriculture and Rural Cooperation, 1989, p. 101-08. bibliog.

Kelly focuses on recent experiences in St. Kitts and on the broad and specific objectives of diversification. The article comments on: agriculture's contribution to the economy; its objectives; earlier and more recent experiences; and constraints. A list of questions and answers further clarifies the subject. The author is at the Agronomy and Research Department, St. Kitts Sugar Manufacturing Corporation. The Caribbean Research and Development Institute (CARDI) also contributed to sponsoring the seminar.

317 **An export data collection and impact monitoring system for the West Indies Tropical Produce Support (TROPRO) project: volume one.**
Organisation of Eastern Caribbean States, Agricultural Diversification Co-ordination Unit, US Agency for International Development. Washington, DC: Sibley International, 1992. 115p.

Describes the goal and work of TROPRO and explains which agencies will utilize the system. The data-collection mechanisms used to obtain specific country data on exports are also described and critical areas for future attention are indicated.

318 **Farming systems of Nevis: report of a rapid reconnaissance survey.**
St. C. Baker. St. Augustine, Trinidad: University of the West Indies, Faculty of Agriculture, 1985. vi, 89p.

A summary of a rapid reconnaissance survey in five sections. These are: an introduction and background to proceedings; an overview with a physical description of Nevis; an analysis of the farm systems; recommendations for improving the farm systems; and conclusions. There are also several appendixes, a list of persons in the multidisciplinary team, guidelines for an exploratory survey with questionnaires, and the programme of activities.

319 **From sugar plantation to open-range grazing: changes in the land use of Nevis, West Indies, 1950-70.**
D. Watts. *Geography*, vol. 85, no. 1 (1973), p. 65-68.

A cautious, if pessimistic speculation as to the consequences of land-use changes in Nevis, over the decades spanning 1950-70. Nevis, formerly one of the richest sugar-producing islands in the Caribbean, is now dependent on subsistence rather than commercial agriculture and is turning, successfully, to small-stock holdings. However, Watts is cautious of overgrazing, soil erosion and the rapid spread of acacia, which may add to, rather than diminish, the problems of small-scale farmers in the island. Other relevant titles are: 'Agronomic possibilities for the development of a cattle industry in the Caribbean (with emphasis on Nevis)' by L. Edwards, in *Resource development in the Caribbean* (Centre for developing area studies, McGill University, 1972, p. 215-24); and 'A review of solo papaya production in Nevis' by L. Edwards, in *Proceedings, Caribbean Food Crop Society*, (vol. 3 [1975], p. 51-54).

320 **Insights into soil conservation in St. Kitts.**
Karl Croma. Basseterre, St. Kitts: National Agricultural Corporation, 1981. 12p.

Discusses different ways of controlling soil erosion in order to enhance the productivity of the land.

321 **Land settlement in Nevis.**
Janet Momsen. In: *Land and development in the Caribbean.* Jean Besson, Janet Momsen. London: Macmillan, 1987. p. 57-66.

Momsen compares different types of land settlements and their relationships to changes in the the state perception of the role of land settlement. She shows how over time, the settlers came to adapt the externally imposed tenure system to their customary attitudes regarding the land.

322 **Pasture research and development in the Eastern Caribbean.**
St. John's, Antigua: Caribbean Research and Development Institute (CARDI), 1986. 47p.

Concentrates on grazing patterns in the Eastern Caribbean for input in the Forage Seed Production Project, funded by the European Development Fund (EDF). The findings should benefit the grass improvement programme of the St. Kitts-Nevis Agricultural Department.

323 **Perspectives on agricultural diversification in St. Kitts-Nevis.**
K. Archibald. Basseterre: Central Committee. National Agricultural and Industrial Exhibition, 1989.

In keeping with the theme of the exhibition – 'Agriculture, industry and tourism: bread winners for the country' – Archibald looks at the avenues for diversifying agriculture in St. Kitts-Nevis and the economic and cultural benefits to be derived from them.

324   Potential for sea-island cotton production in St. Kitts.

Conrad Kelly.   Basseterre, St. Kitts: Ministry of Agriculture, 1986. 9p.

Presented at an FAO Sea Island Cotton Workshop in Bridgetown, Barbados, on 22-24 April 1986, the paper discusses factors which are important to the potential production of cotton in St. Kitts, where no cotton was in production at the time, and points to indicators for future success with the crop.

325   A profile of small farming in St. Kitts: report of a baseline survey.

L. Singh, F. B. Lauckner.   St. Augustine, Trinidad: Caribbean Research and Development Institute (CARDI), Agency of International Development, 1981.

Conducted in order to define the socio-economic factors influencing the choice of farming systems in St. Kitts, this report discusses: cropping and animal systems; the major constraints to production and to marketing produce; the problems which affect the farm family thereby affecting productivity; those farmers who are most likely to succeed; and the response to technology and accessibility.

326   The socialisation of agriculture in St. Kitts: an exploratory econometric analysis.

Frank L. Mills.   St. Thomas, Virgin Islands: College of the Virgin Islands, 1982. 38p.

Presented at the annual meeting of the association of Caribbean Studies, in Havana, Cuba, this paper examines the economic development problems facing Caribbean microstates with reference to the monocrop economy in St. Kitts. It notes that the cost of food imports far exceeds that of exports, and that despite the Government's policy of economic diversification, it still retains sugar production with its high costs.

327   Solanum potato production in St. Kitts and its potential for expansion.

Jerome C. Thomas.   Basseterre, St. Kitts: Ministry of Agriculture, Lands, Housing and Development, 1987. 11p.

Solanum potato is imported but it can be grown in St. Kitts-Nevis. Thomas shows the results of the yield surveys conducted on farmers' fields during the 1986-87 harvest seasons, and also examines the potential for expanded production.

328   Some farm models for agricultural diversification in St. Kitts.

Neville Farquharson.   Washington, DC: Organisation of American States, 1986. 134p.

According to this report, the reasons for diversification are to reduce food imports and to develop alternatives to the declining sugar cane production in St. Kitts. The technical assistance needed for the report was provided by the Organisation of American States, which had the following agenda: to review existing data; to develop alternative agricultural land-use planning models which would be compatible with the national land-use planning and zoning scheme; and to develop a proposal for mapping significant land-use units for the management of non-urban lands in St. Kitts.

329 **Suggested basis for agricultural insurance in the Caribbean: predicting rainfall patterns with reliability.**
Frank L. Mills.   St. Thomas, Virgin Islands: College of the Virgin Islands, 1981. 38p.
The major concern of this paper is to predict monthly rainfall in the Caribbean.

330 **Summary of vegetable production trials at CARDI station, Taylors Range, St. Kitts-Nevis.**
Saxman Singh, S. Parasram.   St. Augustine, Trinidad: Caribbean Research and Development Institute (CARDI), 1981. 25p.
Assesses the success of plant production, plant protection and vegetable crops in the small farm multiple cropping system research project, for the period 1977-81. The project was sponsored by CARDI and the US Agency for International Development.

331 **Vertically integrated cattle-goat operation packing facilities for St. Kitts-Nevis.**
Barry Bobbitt.   Boulder, Colorado: Quantum 1V Group of Companies, 1982. 67p.
Bobbitt describes a joint international agri-business project, sponsored by the governments of China, Taiwan and St. Kitts and Nevis. The project comprises: the establishment of cattle and goat production and a slaughtering/packing facility on St. Kitts; land utilization for producing forage crops for breeding cattle and goats; and a cost/phase analysis of the engineering, technical and management materials essential for implementation.

332 **Vertically integrated pork operation packing for St. Kitts.**
Barry Bobbitt.   Boulder, Colorado: Quantum 1V Group of Companies, 1982. 72p.
The document describes the proposed development of a vertically integrated pork operation including production, feedmills, slaughtering, packaging and marketing for regional and international markets. This agri-business project is sponsored by the governments of China, Taiwan and St. Kitts and Nevis.

Forestry

333 **Development, forestry and environmental quality in the Eastern Caribbean.**
Ariel Lugo.   In: *Sustainable development and environmental management of small islands*.   Edited by William S. Beller, P. d'Ayala, P. Hein.   Paris: UNESCO, 1990. p. 317-42.
Lugo assesses published literature on Eastern Caribbean forestry, water quality and wildlife. The chapter also highlights the environmental quality of forests, and their importance to the human economy.

334 **St. Kitts and Nevis: regional forestry sector study: country report.**
Bridgetown, Barbados: Caribbean Development Bank, 1983. vi, 18p.
Assisted by the Deutsche Forstinventur Service, this study is based on the findings of a regional forestry study carried out in sixteen Caribbean territories. The object of the overall project is to review the state of forestry and forestry-related industries in each island visited. This report identifies projects for forest development in St. Kitts-Nevis, assesses forestry education needs, proposes an extended market and offers other recommendations. Some areas covered are: food policy and legislation; forest administration; forest activities; wildlife and national parks; and forest industries sector. Other relevant titles are: *Some proposals on forestry development in Nevis in relation to a long-term plan for agricultural development* by W. Chalmers (Barbados: Caribbean Development Bank, 1983); *FOA tropical forestry action plan for nine Caricom countries* by W. Chalmers (Rome: FAO, 1990); *Forestry division tree nursery and reforestation outplanting: phases A & B, final report* by R. Ince (Washington, DC: OAS, Department of Regional Development and Government of St. Kitts, 1989).

Pest control

335 **Pesticides and environmental monitoring in the Eastern Caribbean.**
P. DeGeorges.   Bridgetown, Barbados: United States Agency for International Development (USAID), 1989. 2 vols.
Describes the current situation and analyses the needs of individual islands.

336 **Study of the rising rat population in Basseterre.**
Sonia Hector.   Basseterre, St. Kitts: St.Kitts-Nevis Teachers College, [n.p.]. iii, 28p.
The increasing rat population is discussed, and possible causes are suggested.

Food, nutrition and recipes

337 Avoid the bland and sample real Caribbean food.
Garry Steckles.   *The Gazette* (Montreal), (22 January 1994), p. 12.
Steckles observes that in the Caribbean, curried goat can be found virtually everywhere, while goat water is a particular favourite in St. Kitts and Nevis and its culinary cousin, mannish water, is one of Jamaica's most popular dishes. Goat water and mannish water are both soups of goat mutton and vegetables. Caribbean food has recently enjoyed much popularity with many North American food writers, who predict a great future for it, 'following in the footsteps of Szechwan and Cajun'. He explains that 'thousands of tourists while in the Caribbean miss the chance to sample authentic West Indian cuisine which is a pity as the food also mirrors so much of Caribbean history'.

338 Caribbean Diet Digest.
Edited by Dorene E. Carter,   Frederiksted, St. Croix: Caribbean Diet Institute, 1981- . quarterly.
Focuses on a crucial area: the food and nutritional concerns of the people of the Caribbean, and seeks to 'improve the health of residents'. The articles on nutrition, the recipes of notable cooks, the reviews of culinary books, and the announcements of health programmes, make this a useful and interesting item. It is available from: Caribbean Diet Digest, PO Box 191, Frederiksted, St. Croix, United States Virgin Islands, 00840.

339 Directory of food, nutrition and dietetics training programmes in institutions / departments of nutrition, dietetics and home economics in the Caribbean region.
Eunice Warner, Manuelita Zephirin.   Kingston, Jamaica: Caribbean Food and Nutrition Institute, 1987. 159p.
A useful guide which describes the content and duration of courses dealing with food, nutrition and training available in well-established institutions throughout the Caribbean.

340 Gourmet holidays: Nevis.
Terry Weeks.   *Gourmet*, (December 1981), p. 30-32, 138-46.
Weeks describes the vegetation, fisheries, and transportation on Nevis but concentrates on the island cuisine. Recipes offered include: coconut souffle Nisbet Plantation; coconut cake; rum punch; brown sugar syrup; fish chowder; Leonard's Christmas bread; mango chutney; pork souse; and snapper fillets with plantain and peanut cliffdwellers.

341 Nutritional implications of food distribution networks in St. Kitts.
Judith D. Gussler.   Ann Arbor, Michigan: University Microfilms, 1975. 175p.
A detailed study of food sources and production, markets and outlets, transport and service infrastructure, and the way in which they affect the nutritional needs of the public.

Fisheries

342 **An annotated bibliography of seaweeds used for food in the West Indies.**
Organisation of Eastern Caribbean States (OECS). St. John's Antigua: Organisation of Eastern Caribbean States Fisheries Unit, 1990. 75p.

Provides one hundred and sixty references to literature in English, French, Spanish and Portuguese which is relevant to studies of the distribution, ecology, taxonomy, chemistry and cultivation of the marine algae used for food in the West Indies. The findings of each reference is included with a species, subject and geographical index. There are several references to St. Kitts-Nevis.

343 **An assessment of the fishery potential of the Eastern Caribbean.**
Melvin H. Goodwin. St. Thomas, US Virgin Islands: Islands Resources Foundation, 195?. 141p.

This work is arranged in seven sections: a summary of the principal concerns; an examination of the historical, political, social and economic background of the sector; fisheries development activities – past and current; regional trends; an analysis of constraints; a proposed fisheries development programme for the region; and country profiles, including that of St. Kitts-Nevis. In the conclusion, recommendations for the increased exploitation of fisheries are considered.

344 **An assessment of the mariculture potential of the indigenous Eastern Caribbean brine shrimp.**
Melvin H. Goodwin, Euna Moore, Thomas Nun. Red Hook, St. Thomas, US Virgin Islands: Island Resources Foundation, 1984. 117p.

St. Kitts-Nevis is covered in this assessment, in which all member countries of the Organisation of Eastern Caribbean States are included. Topics discussed are: general marine resources; shellfish culture; and shrimps.

345 **The fishery of St. Kitts-Nevis.**
Ralph Wilkins. Basseterre, St. Kitts: St. Kitts-Nevis Government, 1987. 4p.

Describes the current state of the fishery industry: the shelf area available to fishermen; the boats used; and fishermen cooperatives. There are four cooperatives, established in order to provide access to cheaper supplies and a more cohesive approach to marketing. Wilkins indicates the fishing methods which are used and provides some statistics: for example, he reports that 1.2 million pounds of fish are landed annually.

346 **St. Kitts and Nevis: fishery assessment.**
     David A. Olsen.   Bridgetown, Barbados: Caribbean Development
     Bank, 1984. 34p.

Overhauls the fishery resources of the islands, discussing current problems and
offering recommendations. Some problems are concerned with development and
management, such as: the harvesting of lobster and conch beyond sustainable yields;
the harvesting of endangered species such as turtles; the overfishing of small pre-
reproductive fish; and the control of fish poisoning. Annual landings of fish are given,
as are recommendations for upgrading the fishing fleet.

347 **Workshop on the formulation of a regional management and
     development programme for fisheries in the OECS region: report
     of proceedings.**
     Castries, St. Lucia: Central Secretariat, Organisation of Eastern
     Caribbean States (OECS), [n.d.]. 49p.

This assessment of the fishery sector of the islands of the OECS reviews the status of
fishery development, covering issues such as: regional resources; the requirements for
fishing gear and boat development; the harmonisation of fishery laws; and regional
access. The recommendations of the report indicate that a regional management and
development programme would benefit fisheries of the OECS region.

Study of the water resources in Nevis.
See item no. 29.

Water sector programme evaluation: Leeward and Windward Islands.
See item no. 30.

**Some aspects of the possible effects of tourism on agricultural development
in the States of St. Kitts-Nevis-Anguilla.**
See item no. 68.

Transport and Communications

348 **Canto: Quarterly Review of the Caribbean Association of National Telecommunication Organisations.**
Port of Spain, Trinidad: Caribbean Association of National Telecommunication Organisations, 1984- . quarterly.

Informs members of the technological and administrative developments taking place in the organizations of the Association. It aims to reach policy-makers of the Caribbean in order to heighten their awareness of these developments, and to reach out internationally, with news, information and analysis of telecommunication developments in or affecting the Caribbean.

349 **Harmonisation of port tariffs and dues.**
Sherman Thomas. St. John's, Antigua: Commonwealth Fund for Technical Co-operation (CFTC), OECS, 1990.

Thomas seeks, in this report, to reverse the perception that OECS port charges are high and contribute to the sub-region's high cost of living and to the inhibition of OECS trade. Tariff items and operating revenues and expenses are analysed and compared, and a new tariff structure is recommended.

350 **The international transport problems of small states.**
Basseterre, St. Kitts: Commonwealth Secretariat, Eastern Caribbean Central Bank, 1991. 13p.

The major shipping problems of small developing countries are outlined in this short paper, which also looks at the implications for economic development, and the ways in which existing problems could be overcome.

351 **Liat islander.**
St. John's, Antigua: FT Caribbean, 1993. 136p. maps.
A tastefully produced magazine of the Leeward Islands Air Transport (LIAT) – the Caribbean Airline. In his 'welcome aboard' remarks, the Chairman, Lyden Ramdhanny, informs readers about the special link-up service from New York to Grenada and St. Kitts, introduced on 4 April 1993. Fully illustrated in colour, the magazine carries brief articles on: individual islands; Liat's regional offices; Liat's route map; bar tariffs; food and recipes; travellers' tips; and special features, for example, 'promoting Caribbean prestige: Caribbean products and services' on p. 107. Quick facts about St. Kitts can be found on p. 126.

352 **Privatisation gone mad.**
St. John Payne.   Basseterre, St. Kitts: Labour Spokesman Printery, 1987. 9p.
Reviews the establishment and operations of St. Kitts-Nevis Telecommunications Limited.

353 **SKANTEL story.**
Basseterre, St. Kitts: St. Kitts and Nevis Telecommunications Limited, 1989.
A description of the services provided by SKANTEL and an outline of the local activities in which the organization is involved are the main features of this 'story'.

Caribbean handbook, 1986.
See item no. 2.

Geography for C.X.C.
See item no. 18.

Caribbean ports handbook.
See item no. 551.

The year in review: St. Kitts and Nevis in 1988.
See item no. 554.

Labour and Employment

354 Labour in the Caribbean: from emancipation to independence.
Edited by Malcolm Cross, Gad Heuman, foreword by Sidney Mintz.
London: Macmillan Caribbean, 1988. 323p. bibliog.

The editor, assisted by Gad Heuman, and Sidney Mintz, brings together the work of fourteen contributors to this volume. The essays highlight the struggle of labour in the Caribbean to organize and resist exploitation. Chapters three, seven and ten are of particular relevance to the situation in St. Kitts-Nevis.

355 Legal framework of the labour inspection services of St. Kitts-Nevis.
Leroy Connonier. Basseterre, St. Kitts: Labour Department, 1983. 11p.

Outlines the relevant Acts and Regulations relating to the labour inspection service, and assesses and explains some of the legal issues raised. This paper was presented at a seminar for labour inspectors held at Castries, St. Lucia, 18-29 April 1983.

356 Unemployment in St. Kitts.
Michael Blake. Basseterre, St. Kitts: St. Kitts-Nevis Teachers Training College, [n.d.]. 17p.

Blake analyses the unemployment situation, looking at its impact on society and economy, and at possible causes. Recommendations and projections are given.

357 Union holds first training workshop for 1994.
Sandra Massiah. *The Labour Spokesman*, vol. 36, no. 79 (26 March 1994), p. 1, 16.

Conducted under the auspices of the St. Kitts-Nevis Trades and Labour Union and sponsored by the Commonwealth Trade Union Council (CTUC), with the theme 'Train the trainers', the workshop described here was held on 21-25 March 1994. The aims of the CTUC project are: to help to further trade union education; to develop further the skills of trade union educators; to develop the writing skills of participants; to produce simple and easy-to-use education material; and to develop a pool of trade union educators. The proceedings of the workshop can be obtained from the St. Kitts-Nevis Trades and Labour Union, Basseterre, St. Kitts.

Situations in St. Kitts-Nevis that promote migration: a predictive model.
See item no. 140.

St. Kitts-Nevis: description of national legislation relating to natural resources management.
See item no. 250.

Critical look at the human resource in the sugar industry – the monoculture economy of St. Kitts.
See item no. 295.

Caribbean Congress of Labour: Labour Viewpoint.
See item no. 514.

Environment

General and regional

358 **The changing world environment with special reference to small states.**
Compton Bourne.   Basseterre, St. Kitts: Commonwealth Secretariat, Eastern Caribbean Central Bank, 1991. 24p.

The author identifies some of the major developments and trends and indicates their possible implications for small states. The main features reviewed are: population and economic growth; distribution; production; international trade; international finance; the environment; and politics. Bourne concludes that the changing world environment signals to small states the need for fundamental rethinking of economic development policies, and that small nations may best advance their separate interests by acting in concert. Professor Bourne is Pro- Vice-Chancellor and Deputy Principal of the University of the West Indies, St. Augustine.

359 **Ecocentrism not anthropocentrism.**
C. M. Hope. *Caribbean Contact*, vol. 20, no. 3 (May 1994), p. 3.

The editor challenges Caribbean Christians and the world at large to embrace the issue of caring for the environment and sustainable development with deep commitment. He acknowledges the problems caused by situations of extreme poverty, the lack of economic growth and the difficulties of structural adjustment programmes, and is aware of the 'special environmental problems' of small islands. He calls for a completely new outlook on environmental issues in order to foster 'spiritual resources to go through the sacrifices necessary for survival'. Other contributions in the same issue include: 'People: the key to sustainable development', by Margaret Gill; 'One with the environment', by Desrey Fox; 'Sustainable energy in the Caribbean – possibilities for the future', by Professor Oliver Headley; 'CANARI assists sustainability of the Caribbean', by Janice Cumberbatch; 'Management of our seas', by Kenneth Atherley; 'Refuse Generation by a Caribbean throw-away society', by

Chris Griffith; and 'A theology of creation explored', by Rev. William Watty. The issue constitutes a substantial offering to the cause of environmental concerns.

360   **Environmental agenda for the 1990's: a synthesis of the Eastern Caribbean Country environmental profile series.**
Washington, DC: Island Resources Foundation, 1991. 71p.
A general summary of the key environmental issues and problems identified in six Caribbean countries, including St. Kitts-Nevis, presented within an Eastern Caribbean context. The publication also highlights recommendations and guidelines common to all six countries, thereby providing an updated and organized framework for necessary changes in environmental policies and resource management programmes in targeted countries.

361   **Environmental problems and opportunities in small open economies.**
Naresh C. Singh.   Basseterre, St. Kitts: Commonwealth Secretariat, Eastern Caribbean Central Bank, 1991. 20p.
Examines the environmental problems of small States and discusses the factors which make them particularly vulnerable to, and in some cases incapable of dealing with, certain problems. Singh identifies opportunities and measures which these States, the Commonwealth and the wider international community might address, and also sets out a definition of small States and an agenda for action.

362   **Island environments and development.**
Christopher Howell, E. Towle.   St. Thomas, US Virgin Islands: Islands Resources Foundation, 1976. 124p. maps.
This far-reaching work studies the exploitation of mineral resources; the management of man-made resources and the disposal of waste; the management of natural renewable resources (including water, soil, flora and fauna); the conservation of areas of outstanding aesthetic beauty or scientific value; and the preservation of historical sites and other cultural property. Recommendations are given at the end of each section.

363   **Nevis resource assessment and zoning plan.**
I. R. Corker.   Charlestown, Nevis: Land Use Department, 1988. 64p. maps. bibliog.
The work is in two parts. Part one summarizes the island's physical resources, its climate, geology and soils, and its land use, and is intended to provide basic data for making planning decisions. Part two contains the zoning plan for Nevis and presents the information needed for physical planning to the year 2000. Appendixes give data on rainfall and on land suitability classification, and separate maps of soils, land use, and planning zones are included.

364 **St. Kitts-Nevis country environmental profile.**
Valdemar Warner, et al.   Washington, DC: Caribbean Conservation
Association, Islands Resources Foundation, 1991. 252p. maps, bibliog.

Edited by Judith A. Towle, the introductory chapter of this publication gives the
background to the general environmental setting of St. Kitts-Nevis, and reviews the
historical, economical, and social context within which environmental decision-
making must take place. The work goes on to examine a broad spectrum of sector-
specific environmental/developmental topics, for example: marine and terrestrial
systems; parks and protected areas; wildlife; land use planning; agriculture; industry;
energy; and institutional capabilities. Issues, problems and recommendations are
presented within each sector and an extensive bibliography is provided. In addition,
there are forty tables and fifty-nine figures. Other contributors are: Michael King,
Calvin A. Howell, Ronald A. Williams (Project directors); US Agency for
International Development (Project funding); Rebecca Niec (AID Project Officer);
Edward L. Towle (Project team leader); Jean-Pierre Bacle (Graphics and design); St.
Kitts-Nevis Ministry of Agriculture; St. Kitts Heritage Society; Nevis Historical and
Conservation Society; and the permanent Secretary (National Committee Chairman).

Town and country planning

365 **The South East Peninsular project in St. Kitts.**
DESFIL.   Basseterre, St. Kitts: USAID, 1989. 3 vols.

Organized in three volumes, this full-length study aims at the enhancement of the
total environment of St. Kitts-Nevis. Numerous authors make significant
contributions to all three volumes. In volume one, 'Resource Management plans',
chapters include: 'Terrestrial resource management study plan' by M. Brown;
'Natural management plan: storm water, waste water and solid waste management' by
G. Morris; 'Wildlife resources management plan: shore birds' by R. Norton; and
'Marine resources management plan' by E. Wilcox. Volume two, under the general
heading 'Constraints and opportunities: a synthesis of the planning process', brings
together: 'Proposed land use management plan' by E. Starnes, M. Brown and G.
Morris; and 'Handbook of development guidelines and considerations for the south
east peninsula' by Starnes, Brown and Timmins. Volume three concludes with:
'Terrestrial parks and recreational plan for the south east peninsula' by Brown and
Norton; and 'Marine park and recreational plan for the south east peninsular of St.
Kitts-Nevis' by E. Wilcox.

366 **Town and country planning in St. Kitts-Nevis.**
H. Hansen.   St. John's, Antigua: UNDP Physical Planning Project,
1976. maps. bibliog.

Examines and summarizes what has been achieved in the past in this area, and offers
guidelines and proposals for moving forward.

Housing and architecture

367 **The Adams house in paradise.**
William Howard Adams. *House and Garden*, vol. 158 (February 1986), p. 103-07, p. 205-06.

In this article, Adams recounts numerous tales describing how Walter Chatham built a modest villa on the ruins of the Nevis island house where Horatio Nelson was married. One such scenario describes how eight men carried the guest house, a typical Nevisian house, from the road to its present site on the remains of the Montpelier plantation manor. All the remaining 18th century ruins – walls, entry posts, walks, and stone privy – were preserved, because of the significance of the original house in local history. According to the author, the conditions of history, of volatile atmosphere, and of topography had to be taken into account 'if one presumed to build in a place loaded with powerful spirits both seen and unseen'. The excellent photographs which enhance the volume were taken by François Halard.

368 **Architecture of Nevis.**
Daphne Hopson. *Nevis Historical and Conservation Society Newsletter*, vol. 11, p. 14-19.

Hopson analyses the architecture of Nevis and uses illustrations and descriptions to show variations in designs and the factors which have influenced methods of construction.

369 **Buildings of environmental interest in St. Kitts-Nevis.**
Basseterre, St. Kitts: Planning Unit, St. Kitts-Nevis Government, 1976.

Lists buildings in Basseterre, Charlestown, Sandy Point and Old Road Town, giving addresses and guidelines for conserving the interest, image and general appeal of the towns.

370 **Caribbean Georgian: the great and small houses of the West Indies.**
Pamela Gosner. Washington, DC: Three Continents Press, 1982. 296p. maps.

Gosner covers a wealth of colonial architecture and includes over 200 architectural drawings produced on site in sixteen West Indian countries. There are also photographic records. Some areas of detailed study are: the West Indies setting; architecture – early period and classical period; military buildings; plantations; urban architecture; folk architecture; and religious architecture. Illustrations nos. 164-70 are of notable buildings in St. Kitts-Nevis.

371 **Caribbean style.**
Suzanne Slesin, Stafford Cliff, Jack Berthelot, Martine Gaumé, Daniel Chabaneix, illustrated by Gilles De Chabaneix, foreword by Jan Morris. New York: Clarkson N. Potter, 1985. 290p. maps.

Caribbean style offers information on island vegetation and colours, plantation houses, town houses, popular houses, contemporary houses, and gardens. Both foreign and island influences are reflected, and the section 'Architectural Notebook' provides plans and information on different types of houses on various islands. The architecture of the entire Caribbean is portrayed in over 600 exquisite full-colour photographs. Nevis receives eight references with illustrations of its famous unique 'preserves' and St. Kitts only one – on page 174 – of its mountains as seen from the beach near the Nisbet Hotel in Nevis.

372 Hamilton Heritage Centre.

Larke P. Rodgers.   Washington, DC: Department of Development and Environment, Organisation of American States (OAS), 1992. 38p. maps. bibliog.

The objective of this study is to preserve and restore buildings and structures of national importance and historical interest in St. Kitts-Nevis. Following the introduction, Rodgers describes the physical plan of the Hamilton Heritage Centre, and the management structure. The Centre's place in tourism and the economy is discussed, and ways of marketing and a financial analysis are presented. The proposed Centre consists of estates, the Sugar Mill museum, the Botanical Gardens, and the Hamilton Museum. The work includes lists of maps, tables and graphs.

373 Hamilton's sugar mill.

Neil Wright, Ann Wright.   *Industrial Archaeology Review*, vol. 13 (Spring 1991), p. 114-41. maps. bibliog.

A survey of Hamilton's sugar mill, which is claimed by the authors to be one of the few in the Caribbean which still retains much of its machinery and functional architecture, combining 17th-century layout and practice with some elements of 19th-century steam power.

374 Next stop Nevis: a Caribbean house by Taft Architects draws its inspiration from local sources.

Charles Gandee.   *House and Garden*, vol. 153 (May 1991), p. 132-34, p. 195.

An intriguing story of how Taft Architects came to build a winsome plantation house that marries classical allusion with vernacular charm, on Nevis. The temple and tower design is richly illustrated with photographs by Michael Mundy.

Environmental protection

375 The Caribbean: selected maritime law and policy issues.

In: *Ocean use and resource development and management in the Eastern Caribbean.*   Halifax, Canada: Dalhousie Ocean Studies Programme, 1984. maps.

Features of the Convention which affect the Eastern Caribbean include the concept of the Exclusive Economic Zone, the International Seabed, and the availability of technical assistance to developing States. These issues are discussed in relation to the protection and preservation of the marine environment, to research, and to boundary delimitation.

376 **Coastal erosion in St. Kitts-Nevis: extent, causes, solutions.**
Gillian Cambers. Paris: UNESCO, Division of Marine Science, 1985.

Problems have arisen from erosion and the accretion of sediments along the coasts and beaches of St. Kitts; the causes and possible effects of this are shown in this work, which gives recommendations for a rational management programme of beaches and coasts. Earlier works on this subject by Cambers are: *Coastal erosion in St. Kitts-Nevis*, vol.1: St. Kitts, 1983; and vol.2: Nevis, 1983. These are reports prepared for the Canadian High Commission by Caribbean Oceanographic Consulting Company, Barbados. Some of her most recent works are: *Coastal monitoring in Nevis* and *Sand resources in St. Kitts*, both published by the Organisation of American States, 1988.

377 **Economic zone resources for the Leeward Islands: benefits and conflicts.**
Carlyle Mitchell. In: *Ocean use and resource development and management in the Eastern Caribbean.* Halifax, Canada: Dalhousie Ocean Studies Programme, 1984. p. 53-65.

Analyses the development prospects for ocean industries in the Leeward Islands under Extended Economic Zone jurisdiction, and examines the related problems of tourism, fisheries and ocean transportation. Mitchell identifies the need for effective organizations for fisheries management, environmental monitoring and surveillance, and enforcement. The Dalhousie Ocean Studies Programme workshop was held in Basseterre, St Kitts, 7-9 June 1983.

378 **Environmental assessment report on the proposed Southeast Peninsular access road, St. Kitts, West Indies.**
E. Towle. St. Thomas, US Virgin Islands: Islands Resources Foundation, 1986. 200p.

This report concerns a project to build an access road from Frigate Bay through the Southeastern peninsula of St. Kitts, in order to stimulate economic development in the area. The findings are presented in sections which give: summaries and recommendations; a description of the affected environment; the project purpose; an assessment of the environmental consequences; remedial strategies; and management alternatives. Towle prepared this for the government of St. Kitts-Nevis, with funding from the US Agency for International Development.

379 **Erosion of coasts and beaches in the Caribbean islands: an overview of coastal zone management in six Caribbean islands.**
Gillian Cambers. Montevideo, New York: UNESCO, Regional Office for Science and Technology for Latin America and the Caribbean, 1985. 69p.

This overview assesses problems in the management of coasts and beaches in six Eastern Caribbean islands, including St. Kitts-Nevis. Areas covered are: geography;

geology; waves and currents; coastal description; erosion trends; and major coastal problems and concerns.

380 **Implications of the new Law of the Sea Convention for the Eastern Caribbean.**
Dolliver Nelson.   In: *Ocean use and resource development and management in the Eastern Caribbean.*   Halifax, Canada: Dalhousie Ocean Studies Programme, 1984, p. 19-33.

Nelson's paper analyses the implications of the new Law of the Sea Convention for the Eastern Caribbean, taking into acount legal, political, economic, social and environmental factors. There is a more detailed treatment of economic zone resources for the Leeward Islands, environmental engineering in relation to St Kitts, marine environment and resources in the Leeward Islands, and fisheries and hydrocarbon development in the Eastern Caribbean. The Dalhousie Ocean Studies Programme workshop was held in Basseterre, St Kitts, 7-9 June 1983.

381 **Land use management plan for the Southeast Peninsular of St. Kitts, West Indies.**
E. Towle.   St. Thomas, US Virgin Islands: Islands Resources Foundation, 1986. 220p. maps. bibliog.

Analyses and discusses issues relating to the Southeast Peninsular project. Prefaced by an executive summary, the study falls into six sections: the general background to the project; specific information on the peninsular, its features and potential; land use; economic considerations; legal and institutional elements; and development planning, controls and guidelines. As with Towle's other work on this project, *Environmental assessment report on the proposed Southeast Peninsular access road, St. Kitts, West Indies* (q.v.), this report was prepared for the Government of St. Kitts-Nevis, with funding from the US Agency for International Development.

382 **Management of coastal resources in St. Kitts-Nevis: plan of operation for the coastal resource management project.**
Mervin Williams.   Castries, St. Lucia: Organisation of Eastern Caribbean States (OECS), Natural Resources Management Programme (NRMP), 1988. 18p.

The author describes the ten main objectives which are the basis for the coastal resource management project. The various phases of the project are also outlined.

383 **A new law of the sea for the Caribbean.**
E. Gold.   New York: Springer-Verlag, 1988. 276p.

The contributions examine marine law and policy issues in the Lesser Antilles, including St. Kitts-Nevis.

384 **Report of the Organisation of Eastern Caribbean States workshop on maritime delimitation.**
Castries, St. Lucia: Organisation of Eastern Caribbean States, 1988. 23p.

Reports on the state of legislation affecting maritime boundary delimitation in each island of the OECS: it was noted that St. Kitts-Nevis had recent but not totally comprehensive legislation. The report recommends that each island government should seek to obtain hydrographic and other related training to develop domestic capability in this field.

385 Report of the twentieth annual general meeting.
Isla Verde, Puerto Rico: Caribbean Conservation Association, 1986. 51p.

Marine archaeological resources and the treatment of archaeological sites receive special attention in this annual report of the Association. It recommends the development of model marine archaeological policy guidelines for member states, and suggests an inventory and evaluation of coral reefs and the enhancement of reef resources. Presentations on sand and coastal management and shipwreck identification are also given.

386 Study on the implementation of the IALA Maritime Buoyage System in the CARICOM member states: St. Kitts-Nevis.
Ivan Roman, John E. Mahoney.   Georgetown, Guyana: Caribbean Common Market, 1983. 3p.

Primarily, this study sought to determine whether changes were required to conform to the new IALA Maritime Buoyage System, and to assess the adequacy and efficiency of maintenance facilities, equipment and administrative procedures. A recurring problem is the need to update charts but St. Kitts-Nevis apparently require no lateral aids in their system of navigation.

387 Survey of conservation priorities in the Lesser Antilles.
Eastern Caribbean Natural Area Management Programme, Caribbean Conservation Association.   Christiansted, St. Croix: University of Michigan, School of Natural Resources, 1980. 26 vols. maps.

Each country in the group is dealt with in this survey, whose final report was published in 1982 with 37p. It covers general conservation concerns in the Caribbean, such as ecosystems, endangered species, economic issues, data collecting and data analysis.

388 Teachers' guide to the marine environment of St. Kitts-Nevis.
Sandra Godwin, Samuel Heylier.   Basseterre, St. Kitts: Ministries of Education and Agriculture, 1987. 76p. bibliog.

Constitutes part of a project designed to assist teachers in the classroom to present marine related topics; this particular unit of the project covers fishes. It includes: objectives; key concepts; background materials – information and means of improved use and management; student handouts; and instructions for activities. A glossary enhances the work.

St. Kitts and Nevis: regional forestry sector study: country report.
See item no. 334.

The Southeast Peninsular project in St. Kitts.
See item no. 365.

Education

General and regional

389 **Academic persistence of students and school management in the Caribbean.**
Carol A. Logie. *School Organisation*, vol. 11, no. 3 (1991), p. 263-70.

Logie shows how students and teachers in the Caribbean overcome certain problems and difficulties in the pursuit of academic success. The reasons for academic persistence and the implications of these for other countries are given.

390 **The attitudes of top stream third formers towards agricultural science at three secondary schools in St. Kitts.**
Sherrlyn L. Henry. Basseterre, St. Kitts: St. Kitts-Nevis Teachers Training College, [n.d.]. iii, 98p.

The attitudes of top stream third form students towards agricultural science in three secondary schools in St. Kitts – Sandy Point, Basseterre and Canyon – is the focus of this study.

391 **Attitudes to geography in St. Kitts high schools.**
Gweneth T. Hanley. Mona, Jamaica: University of the West Indies, [n.d.] vii, 50p.

This study reveals that pupils generally display a favourable attitude to geography and that there is no significant difference in their attitudes in terms of sex and school location.

392 **The challenge of educational reform in micro-states.**
Howard A. Fergus. *Prospects*, vol. 21, no. 4 (1991), p. 561-71.
Fergus presents a case-study of educational reform in the Organisation of Eastern
Caribbean States, using data from each of the countries, including St. Kitts-Nevis.

393 **Education: Dominica, Bermuda, St. Kitts, Montserrat, Cayman
Islands, British Virgin Islands, Turks and Caicos Islands.**
Census Research Programme. Kingston, Jamaica: University of the
West Indies, CCRS, CIDA, [n.d.]. 359p.
Volume no. 6, part 3 is devoted to the educational statistics of the islands named in
the title, including St. Kitts.

394 **Education in the economic transformation of the state of St. Kitts-
Nevis-Anguilla.**
S. B. Jones-Hendrickson. *Microstate Studies*, no. 2 (1979), p. 40-67.
bibliog.
Jones-Hendrickson examines the hypothesis that 'changes in the level of economic
transformation in the state of St. Kitts-Nevis-Anguilla are related to the changes in
the previous levels of educational development in the state'. The introduction gives
the author's motives for writing the paper; sections two and three present overviews
of the education and economic systems of St. Kitts-Nevis-Anguilla respectively; and
section four explains the analytical framework. It is a very detailed and scholarly
work with several appropriate tables, extensive notes and a long list of references.
Other relevant works by this author are: *A report on education and training needs in
the Eastern Caribbean* (St. Thomas, Virgin Islands: Eastern Caribbean Centre of the
University of the Virgin Islands, 1986. 157p); and 'Excellence and quality in the
Caribbean educational system' in the *Journal of the College of the U.S. Virgin
Islands*, (no. 4 [May 1978], p. 50-66).

395 **Educational development in Eastern Caribbean primary,
secondary and tertiary levels.**
R. M. Nicholson. *Bulletin of Eastern Caribbean Affairs*, vol. 4, no. 3
(July-August 1978), p. 24-28.
Nicholson scans and analyses a decade of educational progress in the region, from
1966 to 1977.

396 **Educational development project of the Governments of the
Eastern Caribbean through the United Nations Development
Programme.**
Alfred Sangster. Kingston, Jamaica: College of Arts, Science and
Technology, 1986. 46p. maps.
A preliminary assessment which offers proposals for the future development of a
multi-island educational development project, which includes St. Kitts-Nevis.

397 Educational research: the English speaking Caribbean.
Errol L. Miller.   Ottawa: International Development Research Centre, 1984. 199p.

Miller's work is a vital tool for those wishing to keep abreast with the educational research which has been carried out in the region.

398 The effects of certain psychological variables on the academic placement of students of the Charlestown Secondary school in Nevis.
Pearlievan Wilkin.   Mona, Jamaica: University of the West Indies, 1986. 122p.

Students are affected psychologically when they are streamed by ability. This report highlights the educational implications of this and makes appropriate recommendations.

399 Equality of educational opportunity of teenage mothers in St. Kitts and Nevis.
Lorna Smithen.   Basseterre, St. Kitts: St. Kitts-Nevis Teachers Training College, [n.d.]. iv, 42p.

In this discourse on the problems of teenage pregnancy, the emphasis is laid on the educational opportunities needed to aid the social and economic development of teenage mothers.

400 Food and nutrition education: a guide for college tutors in the English speaking Caribbean.
Kingston, Jamaica: Caribbean Food and Nutrition Institute, 1987. 182p.

A long-awaited general guide to the organization of syllabi for a vital section of the curriculum, food and nutrition education. Numerous tables and illustrations are provided.

401 An investigation of streaming and certain psychological and achievement factors in sixth grades of selected public primary schools in St. Kitts.
Wendell Wattley.   Mona, Jamaica: University of the West Indies, 1987. 127p.

Wattley discusses the need for educators to foster in children the right attitudes to school and to learning. He also stresses the importance of the creation of appropriate conditions in schools, and gives some recommendations.

402 **Nutrition lesson plans – supplement to food and nutrition education in the primary school: a handbook for Caribbean teachers.**
Patricia Isaacs, Doris Bamble, Versada Campbell. Kingston, Jamaica: Caribbean Food and Nutrition Institute, 1987. 169p.
This well-illustrated guide is a useful tool for Caribbean education departments and teachers who wish to make the curricula more appropriate and meaningful in this area.

403 **Perceived problems of Eastern Caribbean student teachers.**
Arthur Richardson, Cuthbert H. Joseph. *Bulletin of Eastern Caribbean Affairs*, vol. 13, no. 1 (March/April 1987) p. 42-51.
The teaching problems of Caribbean student teachers are compared with those of novice teachers in developed countries in this article. The main concerns are: the stress problems of novice teachers; classroom discipline; assessing student work; relationships with parents; Caribbean student teachers' inadequate school equipment, insufficient materials and supplies; oversized classes; and sex problems. The implications of these problems for teacher education within the Caribbean are discussed.

404 **The primary education project.**
Leonard Shorey. *Bulletin of Eastern Caribbean Affairs*, vol. 7, no. 3 (July-August 1981), p. 22-25.
This four-year project (1980-84), funded by the US Agency for International Development for the Eastern Caribbean and Jamaica, is described by Shorey, the coordinator of the project. He states its objective: 'to enhance primary school education and the quality of administration and educational planning by concentrating on five schools in each territory in three of the following subject areas: language, arts, maths, science and social studies'. Implementation and evaluation officers, including four specialists in subject areas, were appointed in each island. Resource materials would be produced and a series of workshops conducted at territorial and regional levels were scheduled. Shorey was satisfied with the initial success and he envisaged that the benefits would also reach non-project schools. St. Kitts-Nevis schools were involved in the project.

405 **Provision of facilities for pre-university and first year university studies in the OECS sub-region.**
Castries, Saint Lucia: Central Secretariat, Organisation of Eastern Caribbean States (OECS), 1985. 50p.
The draft of a regional project for submission to the European Development Fund. The proposal is based on government priorities and is geared to the improvement of existing facilities.

406 **Reform in education in St. Kitts-Nevis.**
Arthur Richardson. *Bulletin of Eastern Caribbean Affairs*, vol. 10, no. 1 (1984), p. 20-24.
Reform in the education system since 1966 is reviewed by Richardson. He notes the negative public reaction and passivity, and stresses the need for fundamental change in order to foster creativity in the education system.

407 **Report on the University of the West Indies Distance Teaching Experiment.**

Gerald C. Lalor, Christine Marrett. Mona, Jamaica: University of the West Indies, 1986. 84p.

This report describes the teaching materials and methods, programmes, costs, and the future development of the distance teaching experiment and responses to it. The author assesses the model as one which smaller countries could use to introduce various categories of their communities to the power of modern telecommunications and a new learning option.

408 **St. Christopher and Nevis: education sector survey; and analysis of the education and training system and recommendations for its development.**

M'bow Amadou-Mahtar. Paris: UNESCO, 1981. x, 99p.

Prefaced by a summary of the main educational and training problems which confront the country, the report gives general background information and a brief analysis of educational financing. Amadou-Mahtar also treats the principal sectors of education: general education; technical/vocational education; agricultural education; and non-formal education.

409 **St. Kitts and Nevis educational statistics 1987-88.**

Health and Community Affairs. Basseterre, St. Kitts: St. Kitts-Nevis Ministry of Education, 1989. 42p.

Summary statistics are tabulated for primary, secondary and private schools and give the following data: male-female teacher distribution; student age distribution; class distribution; class size; and male-female student distribution. Cambridge 'O' and 'A' levels and CXC examinations results are also included.

410 **Student teachers' ability to define and produce varied examples of geometrical concepts.**

Osmond Petty. *Research In Education*, no. 49 (May 1993), p. 63-73.

Petty follows the work of student teachers of mathematics in the Caribbean, observes their success in producing and defining geometrical concepts, and presents his findings.

411 **Teaching and testing for excellence: an address.**

Roy Marshall. Bridgetown, Barbados: Caribbean Examination Council, 1988. 10p.

This address touches on a wide range of educational topics: examinations; qualifications; teaching and training; curriculum subjects; courses; teaching methods; and teaching personnel. It was given at the annual awards presentation of the Caribbean Examinations Council in Barbados on 7 October 1988.

412 **The teaching of dental health using behavioural science method versus traditional lecture method.**
Gloria V. Nisbett. Basseterre, St. Kitts: St. Kitts-Nevis Teachers Training College, [n.d.]. iii, 79p.
Nisbett presents the results of research which was conducted to investigate whether the behavioural science or the traditional lecture method is more effective in the teaching of dental health.

Child development

413 **A better tomorrow: task force to study a public corporation for child and family development in St. Kitts-Nevis.**
Robert Halpern, David Fisk. Ypsilanti, Michigan: High Scope International Centre, [n.d.]. 44p.
This work constitutes background reference for a task force meeting, the purpose of which was to consider the possibility of establishing a public corporation for child and family development on St. Kitts-Nevis, and to sketch out the parameters of operating the corporation, if the initiative were considered feasible.

414 **Child and Family Development Corporation of St. Kitts-Nevis.**
Leonie James, David Fisk, Robert Halpern. Ypsilanti, Michigan: High Scope International Centre, Agency of International Development, [n.d.]. 32p.
In this final report of the task force, whose aim was to consider the feasibility of setting up a public corporation to support child and family development in St. Kitts-Nevis, recommendations describing the main characteristics of such a corporation are offered.

Human resources development

415 **A calendar of local and international seminars, conferences and self-development programmes.**
Kingston, Jamaica: Department of Library Studies, University of the West Indies, 1989. 26p.
A useful guide to on-going learning opportunities available in the region and in the wider world, designed to in-service training programmes, especially for technical and semi-professional staff.

416 **The culture of development of the West Indian Island of Nevis.**
Karen Fog Olwig. Copenhagen: University of Copenhagen, 1985. 76p.
Outlines the cultural setting of Nevis, the social and economic resources which are
capable of development, and how a development programme may be structured, with
examples of development activity in Nevis during the 1980s. The report concludes
with recommendations for cultural, educational and economic reforms.

417 **Human resources development in the Organisation of Eastern
Caribbean States (OECS).**
Simon Jones-Hendrickson. Basseterre, St. Kitts: Eastern Caribbean
Central Bank, Commonwealth Secretariat, 1991. 12p.
Addresses the theme of human resources development in the Eastern Caribbean
region, and focuses on the areas of health, education, and science and technology.
Jones-Hendrickson concludes that the microstates of the OECS should allow
themselves to benefit from the flow of opportunities deriving from good health care, a
sound educational structure and the scientific and technological developments in the
rapidly changing world of the coming 21st century.

418 **Human resources in the Commonwealth Caribbean.**
Edited by Jack Hardwood. St. Augustine, Trinidad: University of the
West Indies, Institute of Social and Economic Research, 1970. 13p.
A useful work for the comparative study of the subject with islands throughout the
Caribbean. An article in the work by Bertille Alex discusses the relationship between
the existing human resources problems and education, training and employment
opportunity, and has some relevance to St. Kitts-Nevis.

419 **Preparing the human resources for the new service – Caribbean
statistical training programme.**
Osmond Gordon. Georgetown, Guyana: CARICOM, 1989. 6p.
Gordon discusses a strategy for preparing the human resources necessary to cope with
new needs. This publication brings together papers given at a colloquium on statistics
and the new technologies.

420 **Report on identification of training needs for staff development at
the Eastern Caribbean Central Bank.**
Ermine Spence. St John's, Antigua: OECS, Economic Affairs
Secretariat, 1986. 32p.
Spence assesses the training needs of the Bank's staff and offers recommendations.
The Eastern Caribbean Central Bank is located in Basseterre, St. Kitts.

Islands in the sun.
See item no. 20.
Teachers' guide to the marine environment of St. Kitts-Nevis.
See item no. 388.
Caribbean Journal of Education.
See item no. 521.

Science and Technology

421 **Caribbean Community Countries (Caricom) and appropriate technology.**
Winston H. Griffith. *World Development*, vol. 18 (June 1990), p. 845-58. bibliog.
Offers suggestions for introducing alternative methods of technology and for embracing traditional skills.

422 **Cyclones: improving building construction procedures in the Caribbean.**
A. T. Watson. St. John's, Antigua: Pan Caribbean Disaster Preparedness Programme, 1985. 32p.
This is one in a series of building guides which had to be formulated as a result of the destruction wrought by recent hurricanes in the region. It is an easy step-by-step handbook, which shows proportions and percentages for reinforcing building construction.

423 **Renewable energy trends and opportunities in the Caribbean.**
Wallace C. Koehler. St. John's, Antigua: Centre for Energy and Environment Research, 1983. 17p.
Contains useful findings which were prepared for discussion at the joint meeting of the Human Settlements and Economic Affairs Secretariat of the Organisation of Eastern Caribbean States (OECS).

424 **Report of a seminar/workshop on promoting growth and development in the Caribbean: the role of the new technologies.**
London: Commonwealth Secretariat, 1987, 100p.
Sponsored by CARICOM in co-operation with the Commonwealth Secretariat and the National Institute of Higher Education, Research, Science and Technology, the

117

workshop of the title was held in Port of Spain, Trinidad in May 1986. The papers given emphasized the value of new technologies for social and economic growth in the islands.

425 **Report on the Caribbean Energy Information System: its current and proposed service and activities.**
Mona Whyte. Kingston, Jamaica: Caribbean Energy Information System, 1987.
This is the outcome of a meeting held in St. Lucia on 7-9 October 1987, sponsored by the OECS and INFONET. This work defines the goals, objectives and structure of Caribbean Energy Information System (CEIS), which collects, processes and disseminates information relating to all aspects of energy.

426 **Science and technology policy in developing countries: some implications for the Commonwealth Caribbean.**
Arnold McIntyre. St. Augustine, Trinidad: University of the West Indies, 1987. 25p.
McIntyre presented this paper at a Symposium on 'Economic development and prospects of the OECS States' in Antigua, 10-13 June 1987. In it, he outlines existing and proposed science and technology policy in the area, explains the strategy needed to achieve the proposed plan, and suggests effective transfer methods.

427 **Technological education in the Caribbean.**
Glenda M. Prime. *International Journal of Technology and Design Education*, vol. 2, no. 3 (1992), p. 48-57.
The reasons behind the need for technological education in the Caribbean are discussed and specific directions for the future are outlined in this article.

428 **Technology policies for small developing economies: a study of the Caribbean.**
Norman P. Girvan, P. I. Gomes, Donald B. Sangster. Mona, Jamaica: UWI, ISER, 1985.
An examination of feasible policies relating to technological advances in developing Caribbean economies, including that of St. Kitts-Nevis. This study was sponsored by the International Development Research Council, as part of its Caribbean Technology Policy Studies Projects series. The work focuses on the effectiveness of technological transfer and includes useful tables and appendixes: these show different forms of transfer, and describe the results of the study.

Scientific Institutions and Research

429 **Annual technical report, 1988-89.**
     Basseterre, St. Kitts: Caribbean Agricultural Research and
     Development Institute (CARDI), 1989.

An analysis of the year's projects, activity and progress relating to the St. Kitts-Nevis
Unit of the Institute.

430 **Biodiversity – a quick review.**
     Non-Governmental Organisations: News for the Eastern Caribbean,
     no. 18 (August 1993).

Seeks to explain the meaning of the term biodiversity, which is comparatively new,
but which promises to be a key element of research and study for a long time. The
three levels of organization to which biodiversity can be applied are: species
diversity; genetic diversity; and ecosystem diversity. It will prove to be an important
term for Caribbean students and environmentalists.

431 **Caribbean Research Institute report.**
     Edited by Clara Lewis, Liz Wilson, foreword by Arthur Richards.
     Charlotte Amalie, St. Thomas: Caribbean Research Institute,
     University of the Virgin Islands, 1975. 24p.

An illustrated description of the work of the Institute, and its functions, objectives
and programmes. The overall aim, according to the Vice President, D. S. Padda, 'is to
develop and disseminate social and technical knowledge to protect fragile
environments and enhance the quality of life'. Four activity centres which help the
Institute to achieve its goal are: the Social Research Centre; the Water Resources
Research Centre; the Environmental Research Centre; and the Ecological Research
Centre. Each centre is fully described, and the authors provide a directory of the
Institute's staff and a listing of its publications up to 1987. Although the document is
not for sale, it is of importance and is available for reference in libraries. The first
report was published 1n 1965.

432 **Draft report on the second CEIS user training workshop.**
Scientific Research Council, Ministry of Education. Kingston,
Jamaica: Caribbean Energy Information System (CEIS), 1989. 52p.
Records the findings, discussions and conclusions of the meeting of coordinators of the
user training workshop which was held in Basseterre, St. Kitts on 15-22 March 1989.

433 **Elementary data collection approaches for measuring of new and
renewable resources of energy in the Eastern Caribbean.**
Edward C. Alexander. Red Hill, Pennsylvania: Organisation of
American States, Executive Secretariat for Economic and Social
Affairs, 1987. 69p.
The result of the project entitled 'Human settlements and energy project', this work
discovers renewable energy sources in OECS countries, charts the amount of energy
consumed and projects methods to measure new sources.

434 **An export data collection and impact monitoring system for the
West Indies Tropical Produce Support project.**
Organisation of Eastern Caribbean States, Agricultural Diversification
Co-ordinating Unit, US Agency for International Development.
Washington, DC: Sibley International, 1992. 20p.
A summary of the system recommended for the Tropical Produce Support project
(TROPRO) is provided in this short paper. The users of the project, the criteria for
selection, and the collection and analysis of baseline data are treated. The report also
analyses the role of the OECS Agricultural Diversification Co-ordinating Unit and the
future collection and recording of export data of TROPRO's strategic areas.

435 **National agricultural research systems in the Caribbean: a
regional prospective.**
Samsundar Parasram. The Hague, Netherlands: ISNAR, 1992. 6p.
Resulting from an international workshop on management strategies and policies for
agricultural research in small countries, this document sets out the potential of current
systems. Areas covered are: agricultural policy; management; crops; livestock;
natural resources; regional organizations; crop diversification; imports/exports;
horticulture; the Caribbean Common Market; and the Caribbean and States within it.
The conference was held in Mauritius on 20 April-2 May 1992.

436 **St. Kitts Biomedical Research Foundation conducts studies.**
The Labour Spokesman, vol. 35, no. 40 (30 September 1992), p. 4.
This report claims that studies of this Foundation aim to develop treatments for
incurable diseases of the brain, using the most advanced brain imaging machine in the
Caribbean region. St. Kitts monkeys are being used in the experiment. The project is
being monitored by Dr Omar Khan of the University of the West Indies. Further
information can be obtained from Dr Eugene Redmond, President of the Foundation,
Lower Bourryeau Estate, St. Kitts.

Culture and The Arts

General and regional

437 **Caribbean life and culture: a citizen reflects.**
Fred Phillips.   London: Heinemann (Caribbean Ltd), 1991. 252p.
The author reflects on the social, cultural and political growth in St. Kitts-Nevis-Anguilla. The work is well illustrated.

438 **Christmas sports in St. Kitts-Nevis: our neglected cultural tradition.**
Frank L. Mills, Simon Jones-Hendrickson, Bertram S. Eugene.
Charlotte Amalie, St. Thomas, United States Virgin Islands: The authors, 1984, 66p.
The historical, social, cultural and economic factors of Christmas sports are highlighted. Several types of sports are described, such as: the bull play; David and Goliath; Moko-jumbie (dancers on stilts); Masquerade; clowns; cowboys and indians; and actors and mummies. The work claims that the principal reasons for the decline of the traditional sports are emigration and 'high politics'. The authors suggest that a fundamental change in attitudes towards sports is necessary, as is a regard for sports as a genuine art form that deserves to be preserved. The book is illustrated with photographs by Cora L. E. Christian and John Lewis.

439 **Christmases past in Nevis.**
David Robinson.   Charlestown, Nevis: Nevis Historical and Cultural Society, Charlestown Public Library, 1985. 26p.
This collection of Christmas nostalgia is the result of an essay competition organized by the Nevis Historical and Conservation Society and Charlestown Public Library, in order to preserve the rich culture of Nevis. Reference is made to a number of sports and games, religious activities and feasts.

121

440 **Culture fundamental to Caribbean development.**
P. I. Gomes. *Caribbean Contact*, vol. 19, no. 2 (February 1993), p. 2.
In this succinct article, Gomes touches on what he sees as the heart and core of culture: 'National and regional identity, values and the full mobilisation of creativity among the populations of the Caribbean are the underlying cultural forces on which this era will have to rely . . . culture . . . as improvement in the quality of human relations must have bearing on creativity – inventiveness and innovation.'

441 **How aware are we culturally?**
Al Elmes. *St. Kitts and Nevis Journal*, vol. 1, no. 1 (January-March 1985), p. 2-3, 8.
Elmes voices concern about the culture of St. Kitts-Nevis which he terms as under-developed, unexposed and insignificant to some. This article questions whether the country or the region as a whole has a culture that could be called its own. The whole way of life – fashions, books, music, etc. – is strongly influenced by North America, particularly via the domination of American programmes over Caribbean airwaves. The author offers recommendations for the development of the national culture.

442 **Losing their soul in a dish.**
Joan Williams. *Index on Censorship*, no. 19 (August 1990), p. 5-6.
Expresses the fear that US cultural domination will soon dilute the St. Kitts-Nevis identity. The question of television violence and the effects of American television on the youth are also among the most critical problems facing St. Kitts-Nevis today, according to a report on the 'Problems of St. Kitts-Nevis', in *Caribbean Contact*, (vol. 19, no. 2 [February 1993], p. 8).

443 **Our ancestral heritage: a bibliography of the roots of culture in the English speaking Caribbean.**
Compiled by Edward Braithwaite. Kingston, Jamaica: Savacou Publications, 1977. 194p.
Prepared for Carifesta, the Caribbean Festival of Arts of 1976, this work guides the reader to the general background of the Caribbean, its peoples, European settlements, the plantation era and the impact all these influences. St. Kitts-Nevis participated in this and also in the most recent Carifesta held in Trinidad, 1992.

444 **Tribute to our national past.**
Winston Nisbett. *St. Kitts and Nevis Journal*, vol. 1, no. 4, (December 1985), p. 19-21.
Nisbett acknowledges the meaningful but often unrecognized contributions which a few persons have made towards preserving the culture of the country, namely, the stalwarts of Christmas masquerade culture. He stresses the value of this to future generations and also to the economy of the country. He notes the underutilization of Carnival Village (the area designated for carnival celebrations) and proposes a number of possibilities for its continuous use. The St. Kitts-Nevis masquerade is described in *Caribbean festival of arts*, by John W. Nunley and Judith Bettelheim (Seattle, Washington: University of Seattle, 1988, p. 79-83).

Arts and crafts

445　The Caribbean artists movement 1966-72.
Anne Walmsley.　London: New Beacon Books, 1992. 376p. bibliog.

Walmsley traces the origins of this movement through the vision and frustrations of its three founders – poet and publisher John La Rose, the novelist Andrew Salkey, and the poet-historian-cultural activist Edward Kamau Braithwaite. The Caribbean Artists Movement (CAM) was set up in 1966 to generate ideas on and critical discussion of new directions for Caribbean literature and art. This history tells of the clashes and tensions of the early meetings of the founders with artists and writers such as Wilson Harris and John Hearne. The debates, lectures and conferences are documented, aided by the liberal use of illustrations of CAM's people and events. Despite the serious nature of the book, which contains detailed footnotes, appendixes and select bibliographies, it is very readable, and serves as an invaluable source for anyone who is interested in contemporary Caribbean culture and literature.

446　The living arts and crafts of the West Indies.
Florence Lewisohn, Walter Lewisohn, illustrated by Barbara
Meadows.　Christiansted, St. Croix: Virgin Islands Council of the
Arts and the National Endowment for the Arts in Washington, DC,
1973. 56p.

Barbara Meadows's sketches of original Caribbean cultural objects range from religious art, paintings, and daily life, to musicians and dancers, woven crafts and children's toys. The book was designed to encourage a greater interest in the arts and crafts of the entire West Indies and to preserve those already existing.

447　Margetson's centennial year (1892-1992).
The Labour Spokesman, vol. 35, no. 68 (16 January 1993), p. 9.

According to this report which announces Margetson's centenary, Edward Margetson, (1892-1962), was born in St. Kitts to a prominent musical and religious family. He became the organist and choral director of the Moravian Church in Basseterre at the age of fourteen, and later in 1919 emigrated to the United States of America where he studied music composition at Columbia University in New York. In 1927, he and his sister, the late Marie Evelyn, founded the Schubert Music Society in New York. He composed and published over seventy anthems and madrigals, and wrote items for violin, piano, cello, pipe organ and string quartet. As organist and Minister of music at the Church of the Crucifixion, he raised the standard of church music in the community. At the 65th annual Fall Festival of Music, the Schubert Music Society, which is still supported by West Indians, featured the music of its founder.

448　Music in the Caribbean.
John Sealey, Krister Malm.　London: Hodder & Stoughton, 1982.
44p. bibliog.

In his introduction, Hollis Liverpool (the Mighty Chalkdust) recognizes that 'the Caribbean is not lacking in music' and this book provides an understanding into the origins of the various music forms of the region. It shows how African and European forms were synthesized and how Afro-American music was born, and covers the following: the African rumba; the 'son' of Cuba; the 'bomba' and 'plena' of Puerto

Rico; the 'merengue' of Dominican Republic; the 'belé', 'veiquoix' and 'parang' of Trinidad and Grenada; the 'calypso', principally of the English-speaking islands, like St. Kitts-Nevis; the African work songs; the English soldiers' songs; Jamaican reggae and several others. Chapters discuss various music-related topics, such as: music and religion; music and work; fete music; carnival music; neo-traditional and new music; and Caribbean music as world music. The exercises at the end of each chapter, and the useful glossary provided, add to the practical use of this well-illustrated work.

449   **The potters of Nevis.**
       Erly Platzer.   Denver, Colorado: University of Denver, 1979. 111p.
The potters of Nevis are primarily women and pottery to them is both a source of livelihood and of pride. Platzer traces the origins of Nevis pottery, noting the needs of Africans who were transported to the New World as slaves to express their art. Pottery techniques are explained and illustrated.

450   **Review of post-Carifesta art exhibition.**
       Loran Callender.   *The Labour Spokesman*, vol. 35, no. 46
       (21 October 1992), p. 6.
Callender reviews works of art selected from the Carifesta show and exhibited in St. Kitts later in the same year. Among the works displayed were: Caribbean landscapes with tropical symbols; portraits; abstracts done in waters colours; pieces of sculpture; and oil, pen, ink and charcoal compositions. Callender stresses the need to raise the standard of display.

Island profile: serenity in St. Kitts.
See item no. 10.

Determinants and consequences of the migration culture of St. Kitts-Nevis.
See item no. 137.

Culture, race and class in the Commonwealth Caribbean.
See item no. 160.

Afro Caribbean folk medicine.
See item no. 176.

The culture of development of the West Indian Island of Nevis.
See item no. 416.

Caribbean Times.
See item no. 504.

Literature

General and regional

451 Anansesem.
Edited by Velma Pollard.   Kingston, Jamaica: Longman, 1985, 89p.
Anansesem is a Twi word from the Akan language group of Ghana, meaning 'Anancy stories'. It is a collection of folk tales, legends and poems for young people. The theme of the cunning African spider and his animal-human friends runs through several of the items. Although there are no contributions from St. Kitts-Nevis, the common element of Afro-Caribbean culture can be found in the stories.

452 Best West Indian stories.
Introduced by Kenneth Ramchand.   Walton-on-Thames, England: Nelson, 1982. 186p.
In this collection of twenty contributions, Ramchand introduces the short story in West Indian literature as the bridge between the oral tradition and the novel; it draws on many sources, including the folk-tale, the fairy story, the humorous tale, and the anecdote.

453 Black diaspora heard in 'many-tongued' chorus of memory.
Carol Davison.   *The Montreal Gazette*, (12 March 1994), p. 13.
According to Davison, Caryl Phillip's book *Crossing the river* is a 'spiritually significant expression in African-American and Caribbean vernacular'. Himself a writer and poet, Davison presents a thorough analysis and interpretation of Phillip's book, which was short-listed for the Booker Prize in 1993 and published in Canada by Knopf and in London by Picador in 1994. 'Crossing the River', he says, 'is a sophisticated, sorrowful meditation on the painful dislocations born of the "peculiar institution" of slavery'.

454 **Cambridge.**
Caryl Phillips. London: Bloomsbury, 1991. 184p.
Phillips, a Kittitian, brings together two worlds in this book: the world of England, where the idea of the abolition of slavery is supported; and that of the Caribbean plantation, where African children are sold like pets. This is an unforgettable account of man's inhumanity, and of a self-righteous nation which proved resistant to black religious conversion because of the fear that the people might awaken to the realization that under God all are equal.

455 **Caribbean narrative.**
Edited and introduced by O. Dathorne. London: Heinemann, 1966. 247p.
Excerpts from thirteen Caribbean novelists are presented in this volume, which is specially aimed at sixth-formers and university students. The introduction traces the development of West Indian literature and the use of dialect, and humour and myth in literature are explored.

456 **The C.L.R. James reader.**
Edited by Anna Grimshaw. London: Blackwells, 1992.
Fiction, journalistic accounts, and historical and political writing comprise this collection from James's writings, which should stimulate the student of Caribbean issues.

457 **A companion to West Indian literature.**
Michael Highes. London: Collins, 1979. 135p. bibliog.
Brief accounts of the lives and major works of 106 West Indian authors are given, and accompanied by critical essays. Twenty-two literary journals, including *Bim*, are listed in this invaluable compilation of West Indian works.

458 **Critical approaches to West Indian literature.**
Introduced by Roberta Knowles, Ericka Smilowitz. St. Thomas, US Virgin Islands: Humanities Division, College of the Virgin Islands, 1981. 281p. bibliog.
At a joint conference of the College of the Virgin Islands and the University of the West Indies, fourteen papers on Caribbean literature were presented; this volume brings together these edited papers. Aspects of technique, and the functions of various art forms (music, carving, sculpture, etc.) in Caribbean literature are examined and discussed with examples. Other essays include: 'Sir Galahad and the islands'; 'The new West Indian novelists'; 'Roots: a commentary on West Indian writers'; 'Jazz and the West Indian novel'; and 'West Indian prose fiction in the sixties: a survey'.

459 **Crossing the river.**
Caryl Phillips. London: Picador, 1994. 237p.
Phillips traces the lives of three people in three separate journeys in different times and continents, across a period of 250 years. Nash Williams, a missionary in Liberia in the early 1830s; Martha Randolph, a courageous, aging slave who searches for her daughter in the wild west of California in the late 1800s; and Travis, an American GI

who is posted to a Yorkshire village during the Second World War. It is a well conceived and crafted story with a moving emotional force behind it. Susan Walker writes about him in *The Toronto Star*, (15 February 1994), 'The experience of displacement drives U.K. writer Caryl Phillips'. Born in St. Kitts in 1958, Phillips was brought to England in the same year. He grew up in Leeds, was educated at Oxford and has written numerous scripts for film, theatre, radio and television. Other publications are: *A state of independence*; *Strange fruit*; *The European tribe*; *Higher ground*; and *The final passage*. He has won several literary awards and is writer in-residence at Amherst College, Massachusetts.

460 Daughters of Africa.

Edited by Margaret Bushy.   London: Jonathan Cape, 1992. 1152p.

Comprising over two hundred extracts from oral literatures of Africa and the African diaspora, this anthology includes anonymous songs and poetry of Africa, the Dub poetry of Jean Binta Breeze, and the dialect of Louise Bennett. The work is arranged chronologically and constitutes an important historical document, tracing women's writings down the ages to the present day and giving the women of African descent a place in literary history. It is an invaluable book for anyone interested in Caribbean literature and women's studies.

461 Guns of Dragonard.

Rupert Gilchrist.   London: Souvenir Press, 1980. 223p.

Based on the recently discovered historical fact that Negro slaves possessed firearms during the American Civil War, this work recounts an epic tale of jealousy, passion and conflict, concerning the Dragonard family of St. Kitts-Nevis whose fortune is built on slavery. This forms part of Gilchrist's Dragonard series, which comprises: *Dragonard*; *The master of Dragonard Hill*; *Dragonard blood*; *Dragonard rising*; and *The siege of Dragonard Hill*. Other works are *The house at three o'clock* and *A girl called Friday night* .

462 Historical fiction and fictional history: Caryl Phillips.

Evelyn O'Callaghan.   *Journal of Commonwealth Literature*, vol. 28, no. 2 (1992), p. 34-37. bibliog.

O'Callaghan compares Caryl Phillips' book, *Cambridge* with books from authors of similar form, for instance, Carmichael and Lewis. She concludes that '*Cambridge* enables us to see that there are no "true" discourses, only more or less powerful ones'. She recognizes that the discovery of fictional elements in the type of source narratives utilized in *Cambridge*, does not necessarily alter the power of tradition to which they belong, but maintains that after careful reading of the novel, one will never read other similar works (by such as Lewis, Carmichael, Long) in the same way again.

463 The house at 3 o'clock.

Rupert Gilchrist.   London: Souvenir Press, 1982. 232p.

Set in the American south just after emancipation, when four million slaves were freed, the economy was in ruins, cities blazed in battle, and vigilante groups rose up everywhere to smother the constitutional rights that had been extended to Negroes. This work proves that 'freedom meant no more to many black people than being slaves without masters', and is the first volume in the series 'Slaves without masters'.

464 **Hugo and his friends.**
Simon Jones-Hendrickson.   Frederiksted, St. Croix, US Virgin
Islands: Eastern Caribbean Institute, 1990. 69p.

In this work, Hendrickson has personified hurricane Hugo and followed him from his
birth in St. Kitts, to the great devastation which he brought to the islands, St. Croix in
particular, in 1989. The hurricane theme runs through the short story in part one of
the work and through each of the eleven poems in part two. The author contributes to
the documentation of the destruction caused by the hurricane.

465 **The islands in between: essays on West Indian literature.**
Edited and introduced by Louis James.   London: Oxford University
Press, Three Crown Books, 1968. 166p.

The works of West Indian writers are evaluated by their contemporaries, in this useful
volume of literary criticism.

466 **Sonny Jim of Sandy Point.**
Simon Jones-Hendrickson.   Frederiksted, St. Croix, US Virgin
Islands: Eastern Caribbean Institute, 1991. 283p.

An autobiographical novel, written with much sensitivity, and paying attention to
folklore, humour and honesty, language and local colour, which makes fascinating
reading. Other works by the author include two novels, one novella, three volumes of
poetry, a book on economics and many journal articles.

467 **A state of independence.**
Caryl Phillips.   London: Faber, 1986. 157p.

Set in St. Kitts, this work tells the story of Bertam Francis, a British West Indian who
spent many years away from his Caribbean home. He returns shortly after
independence to celebrate Caribbean nationhood, but is shocked and let down by the
behaviour of his friends towards him, soon realizing that he is now an outsider in his
island home.

468 **A wedding on Nevis.**
James A. Mitchener.   In: *Caribbean.*   James Mitchener.   London:
Martin Secker & Warburg, 1989, p. 402-42.

In his international best seller, Mitchener relates tales from the turbulent history of
the Caribbean islands. He uses an extravaganza of actors – including Nelson in Nevis:
'On a historical day in January 1785, Captain Nelson sailed the Boreas to the
beautiful little island of Nevis to discuss matters regarding the sugar trade with that
community's leading planter, Mr. Herbert'. Mitchener goes on to describe Nelson's
meeting with Mrs Nisbet and their subsequent marriage.

469 **West Indian literature.**
Edited and introduced by Bruce King.   London: Macmillan, 1979.
247p. bibliog.

King presents six essays on the historical development of West Indian literature and
eight on literary criticism of the major writers in the English-speaking Caribbean.

Poetry

470 **Caribbean voices: an anthology of West Indian poetry. Vol.1.**
Dreams and visions.
Selected and introduced by John Figueroa. London: Evans Brothers,
1966. 119p. bibliog.

Poems suitable for primary school children feature in this collection. The poems are
arranged under six headings: people; nature; art; in our land; interlude; and beyond.
Selections from the BBC programme, 'Caribbean Voices', and the Caribbean literary
journal *Bim* are included.

471 **Derek Walcott poems 1965-1980.**
Derek Walcott. London: Jonathan Cape, 1992. 270p.

A selection of poetry embracing Walcott's early works such as 'The Castaway'
(1965); 'The Gulf and other poems' (1969); 'Seagrapes'(1976); and 'Star apple
kingdom' (1980). Walcott writes about the Caribbean and although his home island is
St. Lucia, his poetry follows general Caribbean themes and rhythms which are
applicable to St. Kitts-Nevis. The author has won several international awards and
was the winner of the Nobel Prize for Literature, 1992. He is considered as the poet of
the Caribbean and should be read by all Caribbean students of literature.

472 **News from Babylon.**
Edited by James Berry. London: Chatto & Windus, 1984. 212p.

A collection of West Indian British poems dealing with politics, love, humour, and
the relationship between West Indian and British cultures. Among the poets is St.
Kitts born Imruh Bakari Caesar, featured on page 147. He is a film maker and also
works in theatre and television; his publications include 'Sounds and echoes' (1980).
The editor of this poetry collection, Berry, is a West Indian who has lived in Britain
since 1948. He is himself a renowned poet and critic and has published several books.

473 **Our national heritage in prose and verse.**
St. Kitts-Nevis school children. Basseterre, St. Kitts: Ministry of
Education, 1988. 36p.

A selection of prose and poetry by young people aged from six to nineteen years old,
who participated in the Independence Creative Writing Competition organized by the
Ministry of Education and the South East Peninsular Board. The writings include
poetry which uses a wide range of imagery, and narratives which convey drama and
suspense forcefully. Contributions include 'Don't count your chickens before they are
hatched'; 'Guilty conscience needs no accuser'; 'Drugs'; The 'Nevisian Fisherman';
'This Liamuiga'; and 'Land of beauty'.

474 **Poetry in the Caribbean.**
Julie Pearn. London: Hodder & Stoughton, 1985. 60p. bibliog.

Introduced by Louise Bennett, this textbook encourages students to become better
acquainted with regional poets. Issues discussed include: nature in poetry; proverbs;
preacher talk; the influence of jazz; the sea; and Rastafari.

Literature. Poetry

475 Reflections through time.
Simon B. Jones-Hendrickson.   Frederiksted, St. Croix, US Virgin
Islands: Eastern Caribbean Institute, 1989. 54p.

Jones-Hendrickson, poet and economist, offers here fifty-two illuminating poems of
encouragement for the journey through life.

Sports and Recreation

476 **Cricket: Lewis on the brighter side.**
Mike Selvey. *The Guardian*, (1 February 1994), p. 19.
A description of the third and final day of the St. Kitts versus England cricket tour match played in St. Kitts, in 1994.

477 **Development of sports: speech.**
Kennedy Simmonds. Basseterre, St. Kitts: Prime Minister's Office, 1984. 8p.
Delivered on 16 May 1984, this speech is aimed at the young people of St. Kitts-Nevis, and centres on the development of sports. It stresses the importance of a healthy human resource in the national quest for achievement and outlines the government's plans for sports development.

478 **De Village Soccer League.**
De Village Soccer League. *The Labour Spokesman*, vol. 37 (23 April 1994), p. 13.
According to this report, the League, now in its ninth year, started with the aim to develop soccer skills, with an emphasis on respect and discipline, in the West Basseterre area. A football display, described as an 'innovation into local football' was the main attraction of the 24 April 1994 tournament.

479 **Hitting across the boundary line: an autobiography.**
Viv Richards. London: Headline Books, 1992. 241p.
Richards brings 'a new assertiveness in today's West Indian cricket culture' as he relates his experiences as one of the greatest Caribbean cricketers. He tells with conviction of the success of the West Indian working-class struggles against colonialism and racism, and of his quest to attain a respected space for West Indians within the global institutional structure of cricket. He defines to some considerable extent what it is to be West Indian, and how significant cricket is to the West Indians,

bringing together elements of social morality, political ideology and cultural awareness with his own cricketing experience. It is as entertaining as it is a serious statement of significant social value and encouragement, and will be of interest to all West Indians and Caribbeanists.

480   Nevis: nature at its best.

Carolyn Pascal.   *Skin Diver*, (July 1991), p. 34-35, 185.

Identifies the most popular scuba safaris on Nevis and several reef sites. These are: the Caves on the south west side of Nevis, a series of coral caverns, at an average depth of forty feet; Booby High Shoals at a depth of thirty feet; Coral Gardens, which offer schools of creole wrasse and turtles; and Monkey Shoals where sea-fans, sponge life and lobsters can be seen. Redonda Bank is another interesting location, primarily for the more experienced divers; it offers views of hammerhead sharks, whales and dolphins. There are underwater and other illustrations.

481   Nevis philatelic handbooks.

F. J. Meville.   [n.p.], 1909. 60p. bibliog.

Meville explains: the postal arrangements in Nevis; the designs of the first stamps; the manufacture of the stamps; the reconstruction of the plates; and the classification of the first stamps. Typographed stamps and provisional issues are illustrated, and a useful bibliography and checklist are provided.

482   New issues and discoveries.

Stamps, vol. 195 (25 April 1981), p. 268-75.

Stamps of St. Kitts-Nevis-Anguilla are featured in this illustrated issue, and in regular issues of the publication, which looks at philately around the world.

483   The position of cricket, netball and athletics: a social issue in Nevis.

Hensley Daniel.   Basseterre, St. Kitts. Teachers Training College, 1984. 14p.

Daniel reviews the three main sports played in Nevis: cricket, netball and athletics. He examines the problems associated with each one and reveals possible solutions.

484   Skantel St. Kitts Golf championship: a success.

The Labour Spokesman, vol. 35, no. 11 (17 June 1992), p. 6.

Describes the annual tournament which was held for the fourth year on the Frigate Bay golf course in St. Kitts. One hundred and seventeen golfers from fourteen countries, including the host country, participated from 5-7 June 1994. During the tournament, the Organisation for Eastern Caribbean States (OECS) teams were also selected for the 36th annual Caribbean Amateur Golf Championships, to be held in St. Kitts from 9-16 August 1992.

485   Spectacular floral display.

The Labour Spokesman, vol. 35, no. 39 (26 September 1992), p. 2.

This article reports how the St. Kitts Flower Arrangement Association, under the guidance of President Mary Simmonds, celebrated its twelfth anniversary by staging a flower show with the theme, 'Life is like a season'. There were over one hundred entries, including guest entries from Barbados and Montserrat.

486   **West Indians at the wicket.**
      Clayton Goodwin, foreword by Clive Lloyd.   London: Macmillan, 1986. 200p.

West Indians have brought a new vitality and excitement to the game of cricket, according to the critics. Goodwin examines the trends and events which have helped to shape the West Indian teams, through the careers and performances of leading personalities; these include: Victor Eddy, Luther Kelly and Noel Guishard of St. Kitts and Willet Elquemedo of Nevis.

Caribbean islands handbook.
See item no. 3.

Caribbean: the Lesser Antilles.
See item no. 4.

Caribbean explorer.
See item no. 59.

Libraries and
Information Systems

487   Caribbean Library Development.
Enid Baa.   *Libri*, vol. 20, no. 1-2 (1970), p. 29-34.

Reiterates some of the problem areas with which Caribbean libraries have struggled in developing libraries and the librarian profession. The author hopes for further achievement through closer regional library cooperation. This paper was presented at the Caribbean Conference on 'Sharing Caribbean resources for study and research', held at the College of the Virgin Islands at St. Thomas, 17-19 March 1969.

**488   Children – protecting their future: a survey of Library
Summer/Outreach Programmes for children in the Organisation
of Eastern Caribbean States.**
Cecil Ryan.   Castries, St. Lucia: Organisation of Eastern Caribbean States, in association with the Federal Republic of Germany and the Organisation of American States, 1988. 18p. map.

Based on the findings of a survey carried out in the countries of the Eastern Caribbean, including St. Kitts-Nevis, 6-15 January 1988. The report explains: the conceptualization of the survey; its execution; the findings; proposals for new action; and prospects for existing programmes and for the Natural Resources Management Project. Six useful appendixes include a directory of potential resource personnel and their particular area of expertise. The general aim of the survey is 'to enhance the position of the Natural Resource Management Programme to assist Public Libraries and volunteer persons to build and maintain an awareness among young people, of the importance of various natural resources to the sustainable development of their countries'. It is a project that has vision and promise.

489 **Information technology and lifelong education for librarians in the Caribbean.**

Peter Moll. *Association of Caribbean University, Research and Informational Libraries (ACURIL)*, 17th Proceedings, (1987), p. 112-20.

Moll outlines existing information systems in the region and discusses how even libraries and librarians in the smallest islands could benefit from the 'wave of information technology'. The paper expresses the belief that the Caribbean has comparative advantages which could make the region one of the information centres of the world. Also of relevance is Simon Jones-Hendrickson's: 'Information for outreach groups and action research in the Caribbean'; and 'The sharing and dissemination of information' from *Research and documentation in the development sciences in the English speaking Caribbean* (edited by J. E. Green, Carol Collins. Kingston, Jamaica: Institute of Social and Economic Research, University of the West Indies, 1977. p. 141-152).

490 **A need for church libraries.**

Joan Brathwaite. *Caribbean Contact*, vol. 19, no. 6 (June 1993), p. 20.

Brathwaite lists and describes the well known theological libraries in the Caribbean, but stresses the general need of church and church-related libraries to serve church members and other persons who are not necessarily studying in theological seminaries. She describes the Caribbean Conference of Churches Documentation Centre, which was established in Barbados in 1981, but is intended to serve the entire Caribbean area, including St. Kitts-Nevis. With a collection of 3,000 volumes, it offers a library loan service, newspaper clippings service and handles information requests. However, the author strongly urges local churches to set up church libraries according to their needs, discussing the benefits to clergy, church educators, adults and children, and also offering basic guidelines.

491 **New technology in library and information centres in Latin America and the Caribbean: information and development – focus on the Organisation of Eastern Caribbean States (OECS) sub-region.**

Claudette de Freitas. St. John's, Antigua: OECS, Economic Affairs Secretariat, 1993. 24p.

Tells how technological developments in computing and telecommunications have enhanced the role of the library and librarian in the economic and social development of their countries. Experiences with information systems in OECS countries are described and recommendations for developing and sustaining regional information systems are offered.

492 **The place of statistics in a national/regional information system.**

Sandra John. Castries, St. Lucia: OECS, INFONET, 1989. 6p.

A paper given at a colloquium on statistics and the new technologies. It stresses the need for expertise in recording and handling statistical data with modern and efficient machines at a national level, in order to participate fully in regional cooperation schemes for the sharing and dissemination of information.

493 **Proposal: debt recording and management system.**
Pauline Oswitch. Ottawa: International Development Research
Centre (IDRC), Commonwealth Fund for Technical Co-operation
(CFTC), 1987. 22p.

Oswitch examines this sub-regional system (for a group of seven countries in the
Eastern Caribbean), which was designed to support the application of the
Commonwealth Secretariat debt recording and management system. The Eastern
Caribbean Central Bank in St. Christopher-Nevis is the co-ordination agency,
integrating records for the region.

494 **The role of the Library School in continuing education with
special reference to developing countries.**
Daphne Douglas. *Association of Caribbean University, Research
and Information Libraries (ACURIL)*, 17th Proceedings, (1987),
p. 47-50.

In this paper, the Head of the Library School, University of the West Indies,
describes Library School practices, areas of activity, the prospects of developing
countries and problems in delivering services. The conference was held on St. Croix,
4-10 May 1987.

495 **Regional networks in the Caribbean Information System.**
Wilma Primus. Port of Spain, Trinidad: Caribbean Documentation
Centre, 1987. 7p.

Primus outlines the services provided by the Caribbean Information System for the
Caribbean Patent Information Network (CARPIN), and the Caribbean Information
System for Agricultural Sciences (CAGRIS). The conference was held in St. Lucia on
7-9 October 1987 and was sponsored by the information network of the Organisation
for Eastern Caribbean States.

496 **Towards an effective labour market information system in St.
Kitts-Nevis.**
Grace Strachan. Geneva: International Labour Organisation, 1989. 7p.

Presented at a Data Users/Producers Seminar, this paper looks at the labour market
information system of St. Kitts-Nevis and suggests strategies to strengthen the
system. These include: the establishing of a coordinating mechanism; the provision of
basic statistical information on the labour market; staffing of labour market
information programmes; and training. Strachan states that the labour market
imbalance is a serious socio-economic challenge confronting the twin-nation, that
new policies are required, and that political and economic support are essential to the
strengthening of the labour market information system.

Archives and Museums

497 Catalogue of the manuscripts preserved by the library of the University of Cambridge, vol. 1.
Cambridge, England; London: Cambridge University Press, Hamilton, Adams & Co., 31p.

In this catalogue, entry no. 85, under the heading 'Trading and colonial papers', records 'papers relating to the attempts to settle St. Christopher Island; proposals for division of lands there; note of agents for sufferers in the scheme and failure of Nevis debentures'. There are fourteen items for the period 1714-33.

498 Guide to the archives of Nevis.
Edited by Lornette Hanley.   Charlestown, Nevis: Nevis Historical and Conservation Society, 1989. 41p.

Arranged in three broad sections, this work is a listing of the materials in the Alexander Hamilton Museum archives. The index, from A to E, covers in A: Council and Assembly minutes; books and manuscripts; letter/books and despatches; Public Acts and laws (for Nevis only); court records; slave records; ordinary records; wills; treasury and customs; estimates; agricultural records; health; church records; education; parishes' records; reports; and individuals. Section B lists material of the following nature: blue books; Leeward Islands Acts; Leeward Islands Gazette; Official Gazette of St. Christopher & Nevis; Leeward Islands blue book; annual reports; telephone and business directories; newspapers; and Nevis stamps. Section C covers genealogies, and D photography, maps, prints, and programmes of events. The final section, E, of this extremely useful research tool consists of cassette tapes, slide/tape sets and VHS cassettes.

499   **A guide to records in the Leeward Islands.**
E. C. Baker.   Oxford: Blackwells, for the University of the West
Indies, 1965. 115p.

Baker discusses the state of historical archives in the Leeward Islands group,
allocating one section to each territory. He describes the condition of records located
in St. Kitts-Nevis and those located in the United Kingdom. The work is extremely
important to researchers in the islands' history and constitutes a starting point from
which further cataloguing and indexing of archival materials must proceed.

500   **Protecting documents and vital records.**
John Aarons.   St. John's, Antigua: 1989. 1p.

The conference at which this paper was given, 'Networking for the 90's: building a
Caribbean Coalition for Disaster Preparedness', addresses several conservation issues
important to libraries, archives and museums in the entire islands' community.
Another contribution is 'Damage control for museum collections', 9p.

501   **St. Kitts-Nevis: archival organisation.**
Gail D. Saunders.   Paris: UNESCO, 1979. 13p.

Saunders delineates the most urgent needs of non-current records, and gives some
background to archives in St. Kitts-Nevis-Anguilla. Describing the existing state of
the archives, she suggests some improvements which would be necessary in each area
for an archive repository and for its management.

502   **Workshops to improve museum skills.**
Caribbean Regional Museum Development Project.   *The Labour
Spokesman*, vol. 35, no. 28 (20 February 1993), p. 13.

The first of six workshops to be held in different Caribbean islands. The initiative is
designed to help upgrade the standards of museums throughout the Caribbean and to
revive the institutions through workshops training programmes, the refurbishment of
museum buildings, and the reviewing and updating of legislation.

Mass Media

503 **Caribbean media directory.**
Compiled and edited by Joseph McPherson.   Kingston, Jamaica:
Jamaica Institute of Political Education, Eastern Caribbean Institute
for Democracy, 1986. 64p. map.
Provides a list of media enterprises in operation in the territories of the English-
speaking Caribbean. It also offers brief information on geography, people, politics,
government and economic activities. The section covering St. Kitts-Nevis can be
found on p. 37- 38.

504 **Caribbean Times.**
London: Hansib Publishing, 1981- . weekly.
Edited by Arif Ali, this weekly carries abstracts and reviews of films and plays based
on the Caribbean, including those of Kittitian/Nevisian artistes. It has a circulation of
25,000.

505 **Communication for human development: claiming common
ground: a Caribbean prospective.**
Edited by Rudolph Hinds.   Bridgetown, Barbados: Caribbean
Conference of Churches, 1987. 67p.
Problems created by the media for Caribbean people were identified by a study team
from the Caribbean Conference of Churches, Intermedia and the World Association
for Christian Communication. This work examines the effect of the media on
Caribbean people and the problems as identified. The Caribbean Conference of
Churches' perspective on communicating for human development is included. Other
useful articles in this publication are: 'Pirating of the Caribbean' by Rosalind Silver;
'Communications Technology' by Marlene Cuthbert; and 'New Communication
technologies and the Third World cultures' by Neville Jayaweera.

Mass Media

506 **The Democrat.**
Basseterre, St. Kitts: Peoples Action Movement, 1948- . weekly.
A twelve-page tabloid with a circulation of 2,200 which carries general news items and news of government programme and activities.

507 **Final report: Unesco project to strengthen television production capability in the Eastern Caribbean.**
Christopher Laird.   Port of Spain, Trinidad: UNESCO, 1987. 21p.
A summary of the project which was carried out in three phases: a basic training course in television production; the opportunity for trainees to gain hands-on experience at participating television stations; and the supervision of short features. St. Kitts-Nevis was one of the seven participating islands. The report recommends that stations should be encouraged to produce local programmes, and that a certain percentage of local production should be made a condition for private stations to be granted a licence. The project was co-sponsored by the Federal Republic of Germany.

508 **Guide to small unit production of short television features.**
Banyan.   Port of Spain, Trinidad: UNESCO, 1987. 47p.
Guides trainee producers through the process of short television feature production. It deals with: concepts and the choice of subject; scripting; production management; personnel; equipment; and shooting and editing.

509 **The Labour Spokesman.**
Basseterre, St. Kitts: the Labour Party, 1957- . twice weekly.
Edited by Dawud St L. Byron, and with a circulation of 6,000, this newspaper carries news items of general, cultural, social and historical interest. Labour Party activities are emphasized. It is obtainable from: Church Street, Basseterre, St. Kitts .

510 **The press in the Caribbean.**
Joan Williams.   *Index on Censorship*, (20 June 1991), p. 25-26.
Williams affirms that freedom of speech is guaranteed in all the Caribbean islands, and that press freedom is intact in most islands, including St. Kitts-Nevis.

511 **St. Christopher Gazette or the Historical Chronicle.**
Basseterre, St. Kitts: 1747- . weekly. (Continued as St. Christopher Gazette and Caribbean Courier, currently called The Courier).
An article entitled 'St. Kitts and Nevis maintaining unity and winning the battle of the economy', appears in vol. 94: p. 31-48.

Professional Journals

512 Agronomy Monthly Report.
Basseterre, St. Kitts: St. Kitts Sugar Manufacturing Corporation,
[n.d.]. monthly.

A monthly report of the work carried out by the Agronomy Department. The November/December 1988 issue is of particular significance, as it recorded the arrival and planting of sugar cane B88 clones from Barbados Variety Testing Station. The success of the following programmes has been featured in the report: the extended use of promising varieties; herbicide trials; the monitoring of peanut fields for West Indian canefly infestations; the chemical control of sweet potato hornworm; and the cultural and harvesting operations at the Wingfield Tree Crop Project.

513 Cane Manager's Fact Sheet.
Basseterre, St. Kitts: St. Kitts Sugar Manufacturing Corporation,
1988- . monthly.

Deals with all aspects of the sugar crop, for example, production, fields, yields, management, and statistics. Tables, figures and graphs are also included.

514 Caribbean Congress of Labour: Labour Viewpoint.
Norman Centre: Caribbean Congress of Labour, 1962- . triennial.

Reports on Trade Union developments and those economical factors which affect the Caribbean. It supersedes the former publication – *Caribbean Congress of Labour: Perspectives on Caribbean Labour.*

515 Caribbean Conservation News.
St. Michael, Barbados: Caribbean Conservation Association, 1975- .
quarterly.

An invaluable forum for conservation issues, providing news and information for members throughout the region. It reports on the progress of on-going projects and announces forthcoming programmes and activities. It also carries book reviews and well-illustrated articles by experts in conservation and related topics.

516 **Caribbean Development Bank Newsletter.**
Bridgetown, Barbados: Caribbean Development Bank, 1983- .
quarterly.

Provides general information about the bank's activities and serves as an aid in project design and equipment selection for potential investors.

517 **Caribbean Economic Almanac.**
Port of Spain, Trinidad: Economic Business Research Information and Advisory Service, 1962- . irregular.

Edited by Max Ifill, this almanac carries economic and statistical data, covering the Caribbean area and including St. Kitts-Nevis. Related books are also reviewed.

518 **Caribbean Family Planning Affiliation Report.**
St. John's, Antigua: Caribbean Family Planning Affiliation Ltd., 1981- . annual.

Reports on the year's activities, projects, seminars and workshops, giving records of achievements and statistics. It has a circulation of 2,000 and is available from P.O. Box 419, St. John's, Antigua.

519 **Caribbean Geography.**
Kingston, Jamaica: Longman Jamaica Ltd., 1983- . annual.

A journal of geography for the region, carrying well-illustrated articles on all aspects of geography – physical, political and economic, special features, e.g. hurricanes and volcanoes, and maps. Edited by David Barker and Mike Morrissey, the publication also includes abstracts, book reviews, bibliographies, statistics and trade literature.

520 **Caribbean Insight.**
London: West India Committee, 1977- . monthly.

A monthly news and economics magazine, covering thirty-five countries in the Caribbean and Central America. There are frequent news updates on the politics, facts and figures of economic developments and business projects of individual islands, including St. Kitts-Nevis.

521 **Caribbean Journal of Education.**
Mona, Jamaica: Faculty of Education, University of the West Indies, 1974- . triennial.

Lists members of the Education Board, and carries professional articles on all aspects of education, as well as book reviews and bibliographies. It also reports on case-studies in given islands, for example, St. Kitts-Nevis, and is available on microfilm and through ERIC (Educational Research and Information Centre).

522 **Caribbean Journal of Religious Studies.**
Mona, Jamaica: United Theological College of the West Indies,
1975- . semi-annual.
Edited by Ashley Smith, this journal provides a forum for the discussion of religious issues. It also carries book reviews and bibliographies and is available from the United Theological College.

523 **Caribbean Journal of Science.**
Edited by Allen R. Lewis.   Mayaguez, Puerto Rico: University of Puerto Rico, 1961- . annual.
Articles and abstracts in this journal cover biology, deep sea research and oceanography.

524 **Caribbean Monograph Series.**
Edited by Sybil Farrell Lewis.   Mayaguez, Puerto Rico: University of Puerto Rico, 1964- . irregular.
This series provides a forum for the publication of treatises on selected Caribbean topics. It also carries advertisements and book reviews.

525 **Caribbean Nurses Association.**
Christiansted, St. Croix, US Virgin Islands: Caribbean Nurses Association, [n.d.]. quarterly.
Provides news of programmes, projects, seminars and workshops, and of changes within the Association. It also reproduces the proceedings of conferences.

526 **Caribbean Tourism.**
Christ Church, Barbados: Caribbean Tourism Research Centre, 1977- . quarterly.
Publishes lengthy articles (usually with supporting graphs and tables) on current trends on the regional scene and also on individual islands. Attractively bound and presented, it also carries forecasts and book reviews. It supersedes the 1977-81 *Caribbean Tourism Newsletter.*

527 **Caribbean Travel and Life.**
Silver Spring, Maryland: Caribbean Travel & Life, 1986- . bimonthly.
The articles and photographs featured in this publication are devoted to unique vacation, recreational, and cultural spots throughout the island chain. The investment opportunities available in particular islands are also described. It is directed at a sophisticated, up-market readership and has a circulation of 90,000.

528 **Caribbean Treasures.**
Keene, New Hampshire: Close Communications, 1984- . monthly.
Provides informal and objective reporting on the best hotels and restaurants in the Caribbean. St. Kitts-Nevis's 'treasures' are discovered and scrutinized.

Professional Journals

529   Caribbean Update.

Maplewood, New Jersey: Kal Wagenheim. 1985- . monthly.

Focusing on economic and related news of interest to business and government executives, journalists and scholars, this journal also looks at the islands individually and offers up-to-date statistics. In the vol. 10, no.1 issue dated 1 February 1994, there is an article on St. Kitts-Nevis Atlantic Caribbean International Airlines (ACIA).

530   Caribbean Writer.

Charlotte Amalie, St. Thomas, US Virgin Islands: Caribbean Research Institute, 1987- . annual.

A literary magazine which offers publishing opportunities for Caribbean-based writers and encourages the creation of quality poetry and fiction throughout the region. It is available locally from the Caribbean Research Institute, University of the Virgin Islands, and also from regional and international booksellers.

531   Cashbox.

Charlestown, Nevis: Nevis Co-operative Credit Union Limited.

1992- . quarterly.

First published in 1977, but interrupted shortly afterwards, *Cashbox's* renaissance is due to a study on 'The diagnosis of potential feasibility for future growth', undertaken by the Credit Union in October 1991. The journal covers such topics as: facts about the Credit Union; the Credit Union in any language; a checklist for starting a new business; and news items keeping members, officers, employees and the public up-to-date on Union activities. It is distributed freely but donations are appreciated.

532   CEIS (Caribbean Energy Information System) Update.

Kingston, Jamaica: Scientific Research Council, 1967- . quarterly.

Caribbean Energy Information System is a co-operative networking system committed to the sharing and exchange of information in support of regional energy activities. This bulletin provides an update on the activities at the regional and national levels of the system and lists researchers, by country. St. Kitts-Nevis is one of the twelve founding participating countries.

533   Economic and Financial Review.

Basseterre, St Kitts: Research Department, Eastern Caribbean Central Bank, 1983- . quarterly.

Principally features financial and economic statistics, and pertinent news items and articles on matters affecting the state of the economy.

534   Journal of Caribbean Studies.

Coral Gables, Florida: Association of Caribbean Studies, 1981- . biannual.

This journal publishes scholarly articles on all aspects of Caribbean studies, including anthropology, the arts, economy, education, folk culture, geography, history, languages, literature, music, politics, religion, and sociology. Several editions carry articles on St. Kitts-Nevis.

535　**Journal of Commonwealth Literature.**
　　　Oxford: Hans Zell, 1965- . three times per year.

The first two issues of each volume carry critical studies and essays about Commonwealth books and authors; the third issue consists of a checklist of publications of each region in the Commonwealth.

536　**Journal of West Indian Literature.**
　　　Kingston, Jamaica: University of the West Indies, 1986- . semi-annual.

Publishes research in West Indian literature for students and scholars working in that field.

537　**Nevis Historical and Conservation Society Newsletter.**
　　　Edited by Joan Robinson, David Robinson.　Charlestown, Nevis: Nevis Historical and Conservation Society, 1961- . quarterly.

Seeks to preserve the island's notable past by recording lectures, reports, studies, and conference proceedings dealing with its culture, nature and history. It queries resort developments as they affect the cultural and historical image, and announces new books on related topics. Each number carries: the names of officers and members of the executive board of the current year; the chief curators and staff; the Committee chairpersons; and information about the *Newsletter*. It is available from NHCS, PO Box 563, Hamilton House, Charlestown, Nevis.

538　**On Board.**
　　　Kingstown, St. Vincent: Fisheries Unit, Organisation of Eastern Caribbean States (OECS), [n.d.]. bimonthly.

Edited by Michael Findley, the newsletter features fisheries development in OECS countries. The Fisheries Unit was established in 1987 to coordinate the development of fisheries in the eight member states of the OECS and specifically to provide permanent regional fisheries capability. Some of the objectives of this publication are: to emphasize the importance of the natural resource that fish represents; to introduce students to fisheries development in the region; and to offer them a career in marine studies.

539　**Organisation of Eastern Caribbean States – Natural Resources Management Project: News one.**
　　　Castries, St. Lucia: Organisation of Eastern Caribbean States, Natural Resources Management Project, 1987- . irregular.

The newsletter of the Organisation's Natural Resources Management Project, which gives information and news about on-going and future activities. It also lists publications to date.

540　**St. Christopher and Nevis Retail Price Index.**
　　　Basseterre, St. Kitts: St. Kitts and Nevis Planning Unit, [n.d.]. monthly.

Disseminates statistical information on the consumption of domestic and imported foods and supplies. The principal groups analysed are clothing, footwear, food, beverages, furniture and household appliances. It serves as a regular indicator of the movement of prices and of consumerism.

541 St. Christopher Society Heritage Magazine.
Basseterre, St. Kitts: St. Christopher Society Heritage Society, 1989- . irregular.

This magazine aims to bring the concerns of the Society to the general public. It announces programmes and projects and carries reports of its work.

542 St. Kitts and Nevis Chamber of Industry and Commerce Newsletter.
Basseterre, St. Kitts: St. Kitts and Nevis Chamber of Industry and Commerce, [n.d.]. irregular.

Informs members and the general public of changes within the Association, of proposed activities and projects, and of progress reports. The release of 10 August 1992, for instance, carried the progress report of the Beautiful Basseterre Committee, a sub-committee of the Chamber of Commerce; it lists nine buildings completed in 1991, in architectural harmony with the Caribbean style. Seven major developments shortly to be completed were also listed.

543 St. Kitts and Nevis Journal.
Thornhill, California: St. Kitts and Nevis Association International, 1985- . irregular.

Records seminars, workshops and other activities covering the whole spectrum of the educational, social, cultural, economic and political life of the islands. The articles included are informative and critical.

544 St. Kitts and Nevis News Bulletin.
Basseterre, St. Kitts: St. Kitts-Nevis Government, Information Division, 1979- . daily.

This bulletin provides news of governmental projects and activities, including budget announcements, diplomatic discussions, and the progress of industry and tourism.

545 St. Kitts and Nevis Quarterly Tourism Bulletin.
Basseterre, St. Kitts: Ministry of Development, Planning Unit, Statistical Division, [n.d.]. quarterly.

Records visitor arrivals, their methods of travel and their home countries. Statistical tables show arrivals by place of stay, usual residence, and yacht and cruise arrivals for the period under review.

546 St. Kitts and Nevis Tourist Guide.
St. John's, Antigua: St. Kitts-Nevis Tourist Board, FT International, [n.d.]. annual.

This is a serious tourist guide which contains articles about the socio-economic state of the country and items of information and interest for the tourist.

547   **St. Kitts-Nevis Traveller.**
       Basseterre, St. Kitts: Pentaal Ltd. [n.d.]. biannual.

Edited by David Gideon in collaboration with the St. Kitts-Nevis Tourist Board. This illustrated journal carries general and specific information about St.Kitts-Nevis. It includes a calendar of events, some historical background, facts about Nevis, and a list and description of the shops. It also provides information on: carnivals, watersports, nightlife and island cuisine.

Encyclopaedias, Directories and Handbooks

548 Agricultural research directory.
Robert Webb, Walter Knansenberger, Houston Holder.   St. Thomas, US Virgin Islands: The College of the Virgin Islands, Eastern Caribbean Centre, 1986. 98p.

An alphabetical listing of organizations and individuals involved in agricultural research and development in Eastern (and other regionally selected) Caribbean countries.

549 Annual digest of statistics.
St. John's, Antigua: Organisation of Eastern Caribbean States, 1985. 98p.

Presents a range of Caribbean statistics, covering socio-economic developments for 1984. It is published annually, and provides a useful tool for comparing statistics between the islands of the OECS.

550 Caribbean business directory.
Jeremy Taylor.   St. John's, Antigua: Caribbean Publishing, 1991. 264p.

This directory consists of the names, addresses, telephone numbers and range of services provided by merchants and companies. It also incorporates the Caribbean yellow pages.

551 Caribbean Ports Handbook.
Kingston, Jamaica: Caribbean Shipping Association, 1991- . annual.

Lists ports and shipping agents in the Caribbean and describes the ports facilities available on each island.

552   **Directory of publishers, printers and book sellers in the Caribbean Community.**
Edited by I. Dianand, compiled by C. Collins.   Georgetown, Guyana: Information and Documentation Section, Caribbean Community Secretariat, 1980. 33p.

The names and addresses of publishers, printers, booksellers and bookstores are given. There is also a country-by-country listing, St. Kitts-Nevis falling on p. 33.

553   **Eastern Caribbean directory of technical assistance and information programmes for the private sector.**
Resource Industries Ltd.   Bridgetown, Barbados: Caribbean Community Secretariat, 1990. 46p.

Users are guided to services in management and employee training, in overseas market intelligence, in project proposal writing, and in plant operations. A companion to the *Eastern Caribbean financing directory*, this work provides a compendium of the sources of technical assistance that are available.

554   **The year in review: St. Kitts and Nevis in 1988.**
Alister Hector.   Basseterre, St. Kitts: St. Kitts-Nevis Government, 1989. 117p.

Reviews the progress of government sectors annually and carries such items as: sittings of the National Assembly and the Nevis Assembly; progress in development; finance; trade and industry; communication; tourism; health; education; agriculture; women's affairs; home affairs; foreign affairs; community affairs; and sport. The report concludes 'with an air of optimism' pervading the country with the Rt. Hon. Kennedy Simmonds at the helm. Well-illustrated, it is published annually, and it would be interesting to compare this issue with the reviews of the last two years. Reviews for the current year can be obtained from: Public Relations Department, Government Headquarters, Basseterre, St. Kitts.

Abstracts and Bibliographies

555 Bibliography from: Country environmental profile.
Caribbean Conservation Association. Island Resources Foundation. St.
Christopher Heritage Society. Nevis Historical and Conservation
Society.   Estate Nazareth, St. Thomas, US Virgin Islands: US Agency
for International Development, 1991. 22 of 277p.

An up-to-date and comprehensive listing of source materials dealing with resource
development and environmental management in St. Kitts-Nevis. It gives author, title,
publisher and date of publication, but there is no pagination nor annotation. A revised
version of the earlier 1987 edition, it is published as part of the St. Kitts-Nevis
Country Environmental Profile. (It can be obtained from the Caribbean Headquarters
of Island Resources Foundation, 6296 Estate Nazareth, St. Thomas, US Virgin
Islands).

**556 A bibliographical guide to the law in the Commonwealth
Caribbean.**
Compiled by Keith Patchett, Valerie Jenkins.   Mona, Jamaica:
Institute of Social and Economic Research and the Faculty of Law,
University of the West Indies, 1973. 80p. (Law and Society in the
Caribbean, no. 2).

Lists primary sources, including law reports, legislation, official sources and
periodicals for the region in general as well as for individual countries. Secondary
sources, such as legal histories, bibliographies and general legal works, are also
listed, enhancing the value of this guide for researchers.

557 **Cagrindex: abstracts of the agricultural literature of the Caribbean.**
Caribbean Information System for the Agricultural Sciences (CAGRIS). St. Augustine, Trinidad: The Main Library, University of the West Indies, 198?.

Covers agriculture, agricultural education, and literature surveys of the general Caribbean region, as well as of specific islands.

558 **Carindex: Social Sciences and the Humanities.**
St. Augustine, Trinidad: University of the West Indies, 1977- . monthly.

This monthly publication indexes published works and significant articles relating to Caribbean social sciences. A list of the periodicals and newspapers indexed is given and St. Kitts-Nevis is significantly represented. This journal was known as *Carindex: Social Sciences* until 1982.

559 **CarisPlan Abstracts (Caribbean Information System for Economic and Social Planning).**
St. Augustine, Trinidad: The Main Library, University of the West Indies, and the United Nations. 1987- . monthly.

Publishes the abstracts of journal articles and books in the field of Caribbean social sciences.

560 **Complete Caribbeana, 1900-1975: a bibliographical guide to scholarly literature, 4 vols.**
Lambros Comitas. Gainesville, Florida: University of Florida, 1977. 339p.

An established bibliographical source for Caribbean material published in the 19th and 20th centuries, this guide is arranged in subject categories and lists over two hundred and fifty items relating to St. Kitts-Nevis. It updates Comitas' *A topical bibliography*, first published in 1968.

561 **Fishery management.**
St. John's, Antigua: Organisation of Eastern Caribbean States (OECS), Economic Affairs Secretariat (EAS), 1992. 15p. (Select Bibliography no. 10).

A listing of OECS holdings relating to fishery management. It is arranged by database master file number, and accompanied by an alphabetical subject index.

562   **Infonet Current Awareness Bulletin.**
Castries, St. Lucia: Organisation of Eastern Caribbean States,
1987- . monthly.

Lists the output of the regional database and covers economics, agriculture, trade, industry, tourism, natural resources, health, education, law and international relations. Material pertaining to St. Kitts-Nevis is included and should interest policy-makers, planners, technical and administrative personnel in the public and private sectors.

563   **St. Kitts and Nevis Current Awareness Bulletin.**
Basseterre, St. Kitts: National Documentation Centre, 1988- .
monthly.

This bulletin contains a classified listing of the materials, usually local publications and technical reports, which are received at the National Documentation Centre.

564   **Small business.**
St. John's, Antigua: Organisation of Eastern Caribbean States (OECS),
Economic Affairs Secretariat (EAS), 1992. 33p. (Select Bibliography
no. 11).

A listing of OECS holdings relating to small business. It is arranged by database master file number, and is followed by an alphabetical subject index.

565   **Theses on Caribbean topics, 1778-1968.**
Enid M. Baa.   San Juan, Puerto Rico: Institute of Caribbean Studies,
University of Puerto Rico Press, 1970. 141p.

Doctoral dissertations, masters' theses and other theses covering the entire Caribbean are listed in this work. Indexes to the main sequence, which is alphabetical, are arranged by university, country studied, subject and chronology. There are four entries relating to St. Kitts-Nevis. It serves as a useful checklist for all those whose research interests are directly or indirectly linked to the Caribbean region.

Indexes

There follow two separate indexes: a combined author (personal and corporate) and title index; and a subject index. Title entries are italicized and refer either to the main titles, or to other works cited in the annotations. The numbers refer to bibliographical entry rather than page numbers. Individual index entries are arranged in alphabetical sequence.

Index of Authors and Titles

155

157

Index of Subjects

Map of St Kitts-Nevis

This map shows the more important towns and other features.

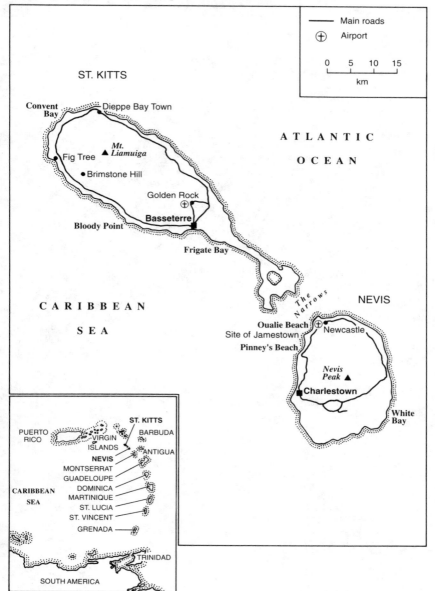

ALSO FROM CLIO PRESS

INTERNATIONAL ORGANIZATIONS SERIES

Each volume in the International Organizations Series is either devoted to one specific organization, or to a number of different organizations operating in a particular region, or engaged in a specific field of activity. The scope of the series is wide-ranging and includes intergovernmental organizations, international non-governmental organizations, and national bodies dealing with international issues. The series is aimed mainly at the English-speaker and each volume provides a selective, annotated, critical bibliography of the organization, or organizations, concerned. The bibliographies cover books, articles, pamphlets, directories, databases and theses and, wherever possible, attention is focused on material about the organizations rather than on the organizations' own publications. Notwithstanding this, the most important official publications, and guides to those publications, will be included. The views expressed in individual volumes, however, are not necessarily those of the publishers.

VOLUMES IN THE SERIES

TITLES IN PREPARATION